"The Dells

AN ILLUSTRATED HISTORY OF WISCONSIN DELLS

Dells Country Historical Society

New Past Press, Inc.

Front and back cover photos, courtesy H.H. Bennett State Historic Site, State Historical Society of Wisconsin.

"The Dells"
An Illustrated History of Wisconsin Dells

Dells Country Historical Society, Wisconsin Dells, Wisconsin
New Past Press, Inc., Friendship, Wisconsin

Edited by Michael J. Goc
New Past Press, Inc., Friendship, Wisconsin
Page and Cover Design by Jay Jocham
Loose Animals Art & Design, Big Flats, Wisconsin

Copyright © 1999
Dells Country Historical Society and New Past Press, Inc.

All Rights Reserved: No part of this book may be reproduced in any form or by any electronic or mechanical means including information storage and retrieval systems without permission in writing from the publisher, except by a reviewer who may quote brief passages in a review.

Library of Congress Cataloging in Publication Data
The Dells : an illustrated history of Wisconsin Dells / [edited by Michael J. Goc].
p.   cm.
ISBN 0-938627-45-7
1. Dells of the Wisconsin Region (Wis.)–history. 2. Wisconsin River (Wis.)–history. 3. Dells of the Wisconsin Region (Wis.)–History Pictorial works. 4. Wisconsin River (Wis.)–History Pictorial works. I. Goc Michael. J.

F587.W8D36 1999
997.5–dc21

99-23999
CIP

Contents

How Wisconsin Dells Got Its Name...   4

1. How the Dells Were Formed...   6
   Eons of Times and a Sudden Flood

2. Native People at the Dells...   8
   A Culture 1,000 Years Old
   Refuge for a Defeated Warrior
   Proud Until Death
   A Hero Who Would Not Leave
   Why the Winnebago are the Ho-Chunk

3. The Working River...   14
   Work for "Wildcats and Alligators"
   Intrigue, Conflict and Violence
   "Hydromania"
   The Great Flood of 1938

4. The Railroad Makes a City...   26
   Great Promise, Bitter Disappointment
   Byron Kilbourn

5. The Civil War...   32
   Heroes Off to War
   "The Best Engineering Feat Ever Performed"
   Confederate Spy at the Dells
   "Soldiers Saddened at Death of Friend"

6. "Wisconsin's Most Popular Vacation Spot"...   38
   "A Place of Resort for Seekers of Pleasure"
   "Holy Rest and Recreation—at Ordinary Prices"
   Lake Delton, A New Style of Tourism
   "Up Where the Pines Begin"

7. Conservation Landmarks...   58
   "Uncountable Millions of Pigeons Slaughtered"
   A Visit from John Muir
   "Every Rock Hidden Is a Sacrilege"
   "No Man Can Own the Dells"
   "I Bought Myself a Sand Farm"

8. Dells Stories...   64
   The First Bridge Across the Wisconsin
   The Hops Boom
   Bloody September, 1869
   "His Words Bite Like Coals of Fire"
   "A Cheerful, Unselfish Life"
   An Auto Trip to Kilbourn
   Ceremonial at Stand Rock
   The H.H. Bennett Historic Site

How Wisconsin Dells Got Its Name

One of the oldest sites to appear on maps of the western Great Lakes region is the "Dalles" of the Wisconsin River. It was identified as a convenient reference point by French explorers in the 1700s, for whom a "dalles" was a fast-moving, rocky stretch of river. The name stuck after the French left Wisconsin, with the spelling and pronunciation Anglicized as the "dells."

When the railroad arrived in 1857, the new village established at the point where the tracks crossed the Wisconsin River was named Kilbourn City in honor of the railroad's president—but locals and visitors alike never stopped referring to the area as the "Dells." In 1931, the city of Kilbourn officially changed its name to Wisconsin Dells.

Today the name is used to refer to the city, the area around it and the "dalles" of the Wisconsin River.

One of the oldest sites to appear on maps of the western Great Lakes region is the "Dalles" of the Wisconsin River.
(Courtesy H.H. Bennett State Historic Site, SHSW)

Previous page: High Rocks from Romance Cliff.
(Courtesy H.H. Bennett State Historic Site, SHSW)

ONE
How the Dells Were Formed

Eons of Times and a Sudden Flood

The work of eons of geological time are on display at Wisconsin Dells. The sandstone in this part of the Wisconsin River channel was formed during the Cambrian Period over 500 million years ago. Originally the shore of an ancient sea, the sand was compacted into rock.

Over millions of years, many more layers of sand blew or washed onto lower layers. Some layers are soft and crumbly, others are relatively impervious to weathering by wind and water. It is this irregular erosion of differing layers of stone that give the Dells rock formations their unusual shapes. While succeeding layers of stone were laid down over many millions of years, the Dells as visible now were fashioned in the more recent glacial period.

The Dells are situated on the extreme eastern margin of the Driftless Area, that unique portion of the state not covered by the last glacier of the Ice Age. The Green Bay Lobe of the glacier extended to within four miles east of the Dells about 19,000 years ago, but did not reach the Dells.

As the glacier melted, it gradually formed glacial Lake Wisconsin, which was about the size of the present Great Salt Lake. Its main basin was 150 feet deep and extended north over nearly all of Adams County to Wisconsin Rapids, west through most of Juneau County to the Wonewoc escarpment and south over the city of Wisconsin Dells. Smaller basins of meltwater formed south of the Dells with outlets in between.

Suddenly one day about 14,000 years ago, the last ice dam holding back the waters of glacial Lake Wisconsin located near the Cascade Mountain Ski Area gave way and unleashed a catastrophic flood. Water poured through the Dells from the main basin to the Lewiston basin dropping the mammoth lake as much as 100 feet, possibly within only a few days. It is likely that the gorges in the Dells area were cut in a matter of days or weeks as the swift flood waters eroded away the soft sandstone.

Probably the other beds abandoned by the river were formed at this time. They have been called "old channels." One extends west from Coldwater Canyon, through Rocky Arbor State Park to Hulbert Creek where it joins the Lower Dells just below the dam. Another gorge encircles Black Hawk Island.

It is these two widely different processes—the layering of sand and rock over millions of years and the sudden, waterfall rush of glacial meltwater—that created the Wisconsin Dells of today.

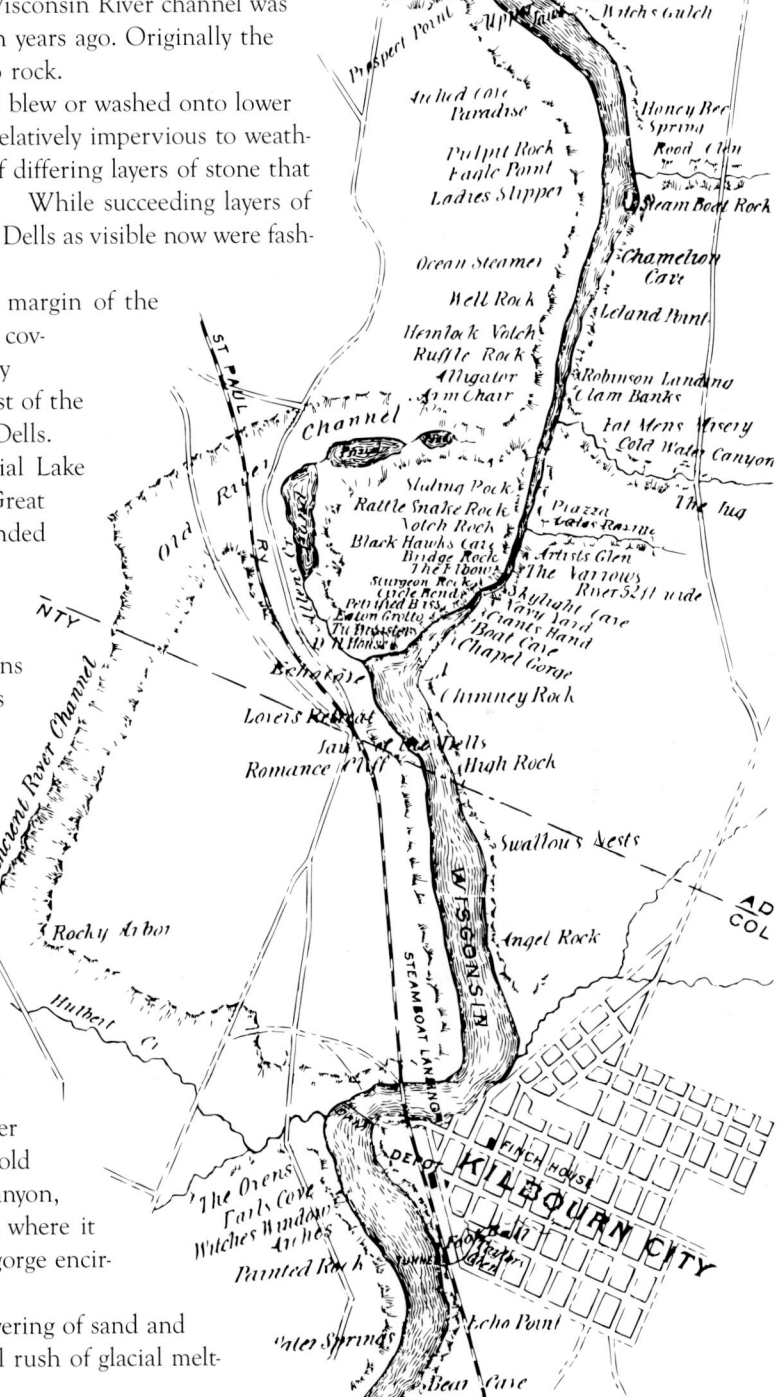

Previous page: Sand deposited over eons of time fused into stone and cut by flooding river water created the distinctive natural beauty of the Dells. (Courtesy H.H. Bennett State Historic Site, SHSW)

Two
Native People at the Dells

A Culture 1,000 Years Old

The Dells area has been inhabited by native people for at least 2,000 years, and probably much longer. Many of them left evidence of their presence in a variety of earthworks.

Hundreds of effigy and burial mounds were constructed in Dells country between approximately 300 and 1400 AD. Although numerous, they represent only a fraction of the thousands of earthen structures constructed by native people in Wisconsin in the years before Christopher Columbus initiated the European settlement of the western hemisphere. Nearly all of these mounds have been obliterated either by farming, by flooding caused by dams, or by the construction of villages and roads.

Among the most notable lost earthworks in Dells country is the "Dell Prairie Enclosure" along Cold Water Canyon Creek. It featured a double embankment with a wall 10 feet wide running from 70 to 230 feet that suggests it was used as a fort.

They are not mounds, but the so-called "Lemonweir glyphs" located on a bluff on the west bank of the Wisconsin just below the mouth of the Lemonweir River depicted fish, deer, buffalo and a thunderbird figure carved into the stone. They too have been lost.

Not all the ancient earthworks have been destroyed. Ancient agriculturists created the still recognizable Hulburt Creek garden beds in the Town of Delton, Sauk County. Built in about 1000 AD, the beds consist of a series of ditches, ridges and furrows designed to buffer frost and for irrigation, weed control, drainage, aeration and soil enrichment.

The Kingsley Bend Wayside on Highway 16 shelters a group of about 20 burial and effigy mounds. There are conical and linear mounds as well as effigies of two 100-feet long bears, a panther with a tail as long as a football field and an eagle with a 200-foot wingspan.

Archaeologists are uncertain what happened to the effigy builders, but surmise they were assimilated into another culture, or simply abandoned the effigy mound phase of their development.

None of the present-day Indian tribes in Wisconsin have traditions or legends which might shed light on the Effigy Mound Culture.

Refuge for a Defeated Warrior

Two of Wisconsin's major Indian tribes, the Menominee and Ho-Chunk, have played significant roles in the history of the Dells. For more than 150 years the furs they trapped in local waters traveled east to the Great Lakes and across the ocean to Europe, making the Dells part of the international economy long before any European appeared here.

The Sauk Indians, who never had a village at the Dells, are important because of the outcome of their conflict with the United States in 1832 and in the legacy left here by their war chief, Black Hawk. After the armed struggle with Black Hawk's band, the United States government adopted its infamous removal policy which stated that all Indians should be moved west of the Mississippi River.

The Sauk conflict also made the name of Black Hawk a part of the legacy of the Dells. After the massacre of his people at the mouth of the Bad Axe River on August 2, 1832, Black Hawk fled into the wild uplands of western Wisconsin. He was pursued by the U.S. Army, state militia units and their Ho-Chunk allies. Twenty-five days later, two Ho-Chunks, Chaetar and One-Eyed Decorah, delivered Black Hawk into American custody. Chaeter later reported that "near

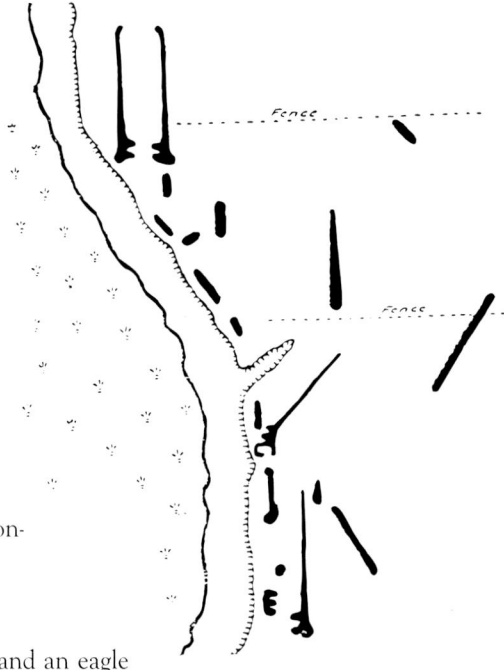

Hundreds of effigy mounds were constructed in Dells country between the years 300 and 1400 A.D.

Previous page: Ho-Chunk people in a traditional-style summer shelter at the Dells, in the late 1800s.
(Courtesy H.H. Bennett State Historic Site, SHSW)

War chief of the Sauk Indians, Black Sparrow Hawk after his surrender in 1832.
(Courtesy H.H. Bennett State Historic Site, SHSW)

the Dalles of the Wisconsin I took Black Hawk." So the legend was born.

Where "near the Dalles" was located has led to much speculation. Is it Black Hawk's Cave in the Narrows, the stone overhang on the bluff at the mouth of the Lemonweir, or even Seven Mile Bluff near Mauston with its lone white pine as depicted by H. H. Bennett?

General Joseph M. Street, the Indian Agent to whom the Ho-Chunks delivered Black Hawk, reported to his superiors in Washington that "The Black Hawk was taken about 40 miles above the Portage, on the Wiskinsin River near a place called the Dalle."

Shortly after his arrival at Kilbourn in 1857, George Bennett wrote that "we saw the Cave where Black Hawk the Indian Warrior hid himself when he was pursued by the soldiers and he was taken but a few miles from here."

On January 28, 1858, Henry W. Tenney, a Newport land speculator who had just lost a bundle, wrote to Horace A. Tenney, "A little while ago I was rich now I am obliged to consider where I shall hide when I see the sheriff after me... I have thought of the cave in the Dells where Black Hawk hid after the disastrous day of Bad Ax but that is too near Kilbourn City." If Tenney had to hide from his creditors, he didn't want to be too close to them.

General Street's report was written shortly after Black Hawk was taken, Bennett's and Tenney's about 25 years later. In between, the tradition that the Sauk leader was captured fairly close to the Dells was well established. Place names in the Dells like Black Hawk Island, Black Hawk's Head, Black Hawk's Cave and Black Hawk's Leap all turned up on the map, along with numerous hotels, restaurants, souvenir shops and attractions featuring the Sauk leader. In typical Dells style, many places were embellished with yarns, as in the case of Black Hawk's Leap where the fleeing Indian supposedly coaxed his fearless pony to leap 52-feet across the Narrows of the Wisconsin.

The tradition that Black Hawk was captured near the Dells stood largely unchallenged until 1988, when Wisconsin's leading Indian historian, Nancy Lurie, brought to light new evidence. Lurie contended that Black Hawk was captured, not on the Wisconsin, but near Tomah, about 46 miles from the Dells. Other scholars contest Lurie's assertion and the discussion continues.

No one, except Chaeter, One-Eyed Decorah and Black Hawk himself, ever really did know for sure where the Sauk leader was captured. Perhaps no one ever shall and that only makes a good Wisconsin Dells story even better.

Proud Until Death

In 1994, the people who were called Winnebago by French furtraders more than 300 years earlier, chose to identify themselves by a shortened form of their original name, the Ho-Chunk. They were and are the largest native tribe to live in the Dells area.

Although they had fought with the American army against Black Hawk in 1832, the Ho-Chunk had not always been allies of the newcomers. Only six years earlier, violence between the Ho-Chunk and the Americans had broken out and "war" seemed imminent. Peace was preserved, at least in part, due to the responsible action taken by the Ho-Chunk leader named Red Bird.

In 1826, the United States recognized Ho-Chunk ownership of most of the southern two-thirds of Wisconsin. Nonetheless, white settlers were moving in and acting as if they intended to stay. Violence began near Prairie du Chien when a family of whites tapped sugar maple trees that belonged to the Ho-Chunk and the Indians killed them. The following year, Red Bird and three companions entered a home on the edge of Prairie du Chien, killed two men and scalped a child named Marie Regis Gagnier. The American reaction was swift and powerful. Regular army units were mobilized, some from as far away at St. Louis and state militia called out. Led by General Henry Atkinson, the troops converged on the Fox-Wisconsin portage and threatened to attack unless the murderers surrendered.

On Sept. 6, 1827, troops commanded by Major Henry Whistler sighted a band of about thirty Indians at the portage.

The Ho-Chunks approached carrying two American flags on each side of their group and in the center of the men was Red Bird holding a white flag. When they reached the river the sound of someone singing could be heard and those who were nearest said, "It is Red Bird singing his death song."

The remainder of the story is related by Thomas McKenney, later head of the Indian Service and a renowned painter and illustrator. His dramatic account has inspired the legend of the "surrender of Red Bird."

"All eyes were fixed upon Red Bird; and well they might be, for of all the Indians I ever saw he was, without exception, the most perfect in form, in face, and gesture. In height he was about six feet, straight but without restraint. His proportions were those of the most exact symmetry, and these embraced the entire man, from his head to his feet. His very fingers were models of beauty - I never beheld a face that was so full of all the ennobling and at the same time the most winning expression. It was impossible to combine with such a face the thought that he who wore it could be a murderer. It appeared to be a compound of grace and dignity, of firmness and decision, all tempered with mildness and mercy. During my attempted analysis of this face I could not but ask myself, can this man be a murderer. Is he the same who shot, scalped and cut the throat of Gagnier? His head, too, no head was ever so well formed. There was no ornamentating the hair after the Indian fashion, no clubbing it up in blocks, no loose or straggling parts, but it was cut after the fashion of the most civilized. His face was painted one side red, the other intermixed with green and white. Around his neck he wore a collar of Wampum, beautifully mixed with white. The claws of the panther or wildcat formed the rim of the collar. He was clothed in Yankton dress, new and beautiful. The material was of dressed elk skin almost a pure white. It consisted of a jacket, the sleeves being cut to fit this finely formed arm. On each shoulder he wore a preserved red bird. Blue beads were employed to vary and enrich the fringe of the leggings. On his feet he wore moccasins. Across the breast in a diagonal position was his war pipe, at least three feet long, brightly ornamented with dyed horse hair and the feathers and bills of birds. In one hand he held the white flag and in the other the calumet, or pipe of peace."

"All eyes were fixed upon Red Bird... His proportions were those of the most exact symmetry, and these embraced the entire man, from his head to his feet.

THOMAS MCKENNEY

Ho-Chunk leader Red Bird dressed in an "elk skin almost a pure white" in order to surrender to the U.S. Army and preserve peace in Wisconsin in 1827. (Courtesy H.H. Bennett State Historic Site, SHSW)

Red Bird was aware of the Indian custom of exacting personal revenge on those who committed murder. He also knew that General Atkinson had promised that the army would not harm the Ho-Chunk if the murderers were handed over for trial.

Red Bird said, "I am ready." Then advancing a step he paused, saying "I do not wish to be put in irons. Let me be free. I have given away my life. It is gone." Stooping and taking some dust between his fingers he blew it away and said, "like that."

"I would not take it back. It is gone."

He then presented himself to be executed immediately.

Instead, Red Bird and several other Indians were arrested and imprisoned. The following winter he died behind bars; some say he committed suicide, others say illness claimed him. The rest of the Ho-Chunk defendants were tried, found guilty and condemned to death, but were pardoned by President John Quincy Adams.

Why the Winnebago are the Ho-Chunk

For as long as they could remember, the people who called themselves the Ho-Chunkgra lived in the southern half of Wisconsin. They met their first European in 1634, when French voyageur Jean Nicolet traveled west from Montreal in search of the fabled Northwest Passage between the Atlantic and Pacific Oceans. He had heard of the Ho-Chunkgra as the "People of the Sea" who lived along the route and who, he hoped, would guide him all the way to China. Instead, they greeted him hospitably and, perhaps, guided him up the Fox River.

The Algonquin Indians who accompanied Nicolet had their own name for the Ho-Chunkgra. They called them the Winnebago. The French furtraders who came a few years after Nicolet called the Ho-Chunkgra, les puans, or "stinkards" after the strong, sulfur smell of the water at Green Bay. The English traders who followed the French preferred the Algonquin name and so the Ho-Chunkgra passed into the historical record as the Wisconsin Winnebago Indians.

They remained the Wisconsin Winnebago until November 1994, when they chose to once again be known by the name they had always called themselves, the Ho-Chunkgra conveniently shortened to Ho-Chunk. It is not a new name. Instead, it is the oldest name of the native people of the Dells area and the first name they gave to themselves.

(Courtesy H.H. Bennett State Historic Site, SHSW)

Marie Regis Gagnier, the scalped child, lived to old age at Prairie du Chien and occasionally showed her wounded head at public exhibitions for a fee.

Red Bird's dramatic surrender ended the war and along with a treaty in which the Ho-Chunk ceded all of Wisconsin south and west of the portage insured the safety of his people for a few more years.

A Hero Who Would Not Leave

Although they fought against the Sauk in the Black Hawk War, the Ho-Chunk were not spared punishment for it. In 1832, they ceded claims to land in east central Wisconsin, including Lake Winnebago and the Fox-Wisconsin portage. In 1837, a group of Ho-Chunks visiting Washington D. C., were coerced into signing a treaty that relinquished all their remaining territory in the state.

This treaty set the stage for another act in the sad drama of American Indian history and led to the emergence of the most important Ho-Chunk leader ever to appear at Wisconsin Dells.

His name was Yellow Thunder and he is perhaps best remembered as the man who would not leave. He refused to recognize the treaty signed in Washington and refused to answer federal summons to assemble for removal to the west. Four times between 1844 and 1873, the federal government hired contractors who assembled posses to round up Indians, load them on steamboats or railcars and forcibly evict them. The wisdom of this policy was inadvertently pointed out by one officer involved in the removal of 1844. "Good God," he exclaimed, "what harm could these few poor Indians do among the rocks?"

Nonetheless, they were removed. When captured and forced to go to Iowa, Minnesota or Nebraska, Yellow Thunder stayed away only long enough to turn around and walk home, sometimes returning sooner than the guards who had escorted him west. Many Indians followed Yellow Thunder, defied the removal policy and came home to central Wisconsin, where they lived as best they could among the growing white population. Other Ho-Chunks chose to stay in Nebraska and, to this day, the tribe is split into two branches.

In 1849, Yellow Thunder attempted to evade removal by buying forty acres in the Town of Delton, presuming that, as a landowner and American taxpayer, he could not be evicted. Yellow Thunder's forty became a haven for the Ho-Chunks and the site of pow-wows and dancing. Even after Yellow Thunder died, Indians continued to gather and dance at his forty. Soon tourists who wanted to see Indians dance started to appear, laying the groundwork for the Dells Indian ceremonials.

After its final attempt to remove the Ho-Chunks from Wisconsin in 1873, the federal government reversed its policy. Although they would not have a reservation guaranteed by a treaty in Wisconsin, the Ho-Chunks would no longer be hunted, rounded up and transported. In 1875, the provisions of the Homestead Act were extended to Indians and many of the roughly 500 Ho-Chunks in the Dells area filed claims to land in Adams, Sauk and Juneau counties.

Yellow Thunder died in 1874. He had lived long enough to see the government's removal policy defeated by his own refusal policy. The Ho-Chunk would remain in the Dells area that had been their home for thousands of years. All the Indian heritage on display at the Dells from the Stand Rock Ceremonial to the "authentic" Indian souvenirs in the tourist shops owes its presence to the man who refused to leave.

Yellow Thunder is buried with his wife, Washington Woman, on County Trunk A, south of Lake Delton.

Yellow Thunder, the Ho-Chunk leader who refused to leave his homeland, sitting in front of a traditional Ho-Chunk reed shelter.
(Courtesy H.H. Bennett State Historic Site, SHSW)

NATIVE PEOPLE AT THE DELLS

Three
The Working River

Work for "Wildcats and Alligators"

In the early days when lumbering was the state's leading industry, the river at the Dells played a leading role in the drama of rafting. Down most of its length, the Wisconsin is a placid, tranquil river but at the Narrows of the Dells, where it is confined within high rocky banks and only fifty feet wide, it can become a wild and unpredictable terror to all who try to traverse it.

Before white settlers arrived in Wisconsin much of the state was forested. White pine was the first timber considered for commercial logging because it would float down the rivers when freshly cut. White pine in the northern two thirds of the state averaged 3 1/2 feet at the base, stood 70 feet tall and grew near the streams. As the Midwest and the treeless plains farther west were settled, lumber was needed for homes, barns and businesses. The vast northern forest seemed inexhaustible.

The first recorded logging on the Wisconsin River was by soldiers led by Lt. Jefferson Davis, later president of the Confederacy, in 1828 for the building of Fort Winnebago near Portage. In 1833, George Whitney and John Metcalf ran the first lumber raft from a mill near Nekoosa through the Dells to Portage.

Between 1814 and 1848 lands on the Upper Wisconsin were ceded by various Indian tribes and lumbering grew rapidly. Timber was floated down many streams to mills which sawed the logs into rough lumber. In 1847, 24 mills were running; six years later that number increased to 100. By 1872, the river's annual output was over 200 million board feet. With no railroads present, Wisconsin River sawmill owners moved their lumber to market by rafting it down the Wisconsin River.

The Wisconsin was a great waterway to float rafts to market except for three impediments. First, there were wicked rapids at Grand Rapids, now Wisconsin Rapids. Next was the almost right-angled turn at the Devil's Elbow in the Dells. Finally, a short way downstream was the passage over or through the dam at Kilbourn. Once these dangers were past, rafts drifted peacefully on their way to their markets as far south as St. Louis.

Lumber rafts were cleverly constructed for flexibility and stability when encountering obstacles. The art of building rafts came to Wisconsin, along with other logging practices, from eastern lumbermen who had followed the trade west.

The basic unit of a lumber raft was a crib. The framework of each crib was started by placing on the ground 3 grub planks about eight feet apart and parallel to each other. On each end and across the center of the grub planks, running the opposite way were placed the three cross planks. All of the grub and cross planks had two inch holes bored through them on each end and another exactly in the middle. The grub stakes were then inserted upward thru the matching holes on each side, each corner and in the middle of the framework. The grub was made of a small oak tree with the root end at the bottom of the planks so that the lumber would not pull through. The grub stakes were long enough so all the alternating layers of lumber were placed on top of them, each with its own hole drilled to hold them in place on the grub stakes. These stakes extended above the completed raft and served many purposes.

A crib was from 12 to 24 courses deep depending on whether the wood was dry or green and the depth of the river it was to traverse. Witch planks were laid on the final course of the lumber and a tool called a Witch was used to compress a crib by pulling up on the grub stake. The rafts rode only some two to five inches out of the water. When each crib was completed, it was slid carefully into the water or on the ice. Then the cribs were attached together with coupling slabs over the grub stakes. Seven cribs commonly were coupled together to make one string or rapids piece of a Wisconsin raft.

Dr. E.C. Dixon of Kilbourn recounted: "I was once on a two string raft as it ran the old Kilbourn dam and the plunge of the raft over the drop was so heavy that the spring poles broke

Previous page: River men reassembling lumber rafts after passing through the treacherous water at the Dells. Boards cut at sawmills upstream were stacked up to 24 layers thick, pegged together into rafts and floated down river from northern Wisconsin as far as St. Louis.
(Courtesy H.H. Bennett State Historic Site, SHSW)

and both front cribs buckled clear under the ones behind them, thus making a raft two cribs deep. You may imagine that there was great excitement at the time and a wild scramble of the men to escape being thrown into the river."

A Wisconsin raft consisted of three strings yoked together. In tight places or fast water, the strings were taken apart so each string or rapids piece could be taken through by a full crew. Such maneuvering was always necessary in going through the chute at the Kilbourn dam and often in the Narrows. After the last obstacle was past, the crew then walked or "gigged back" to the head of the Dells and then rode another string or rapids piece down to safety below the dam. This was a rough hike up hills and down ravines. A fleet could consist of as many as twenty of these three string rafts run together by one pilot. The fleets were equipped with cook stoves and their shanties called wanigans, dining tables and "dog houses" for sleeping. Shingles and lath were often cargo carried on the decks of the rafts. Thus the crew was riding the product to market.

If a fleet started above Wausau, it could usually figure on being in St. Louis in 24 days. Often it took longer if the water was too high to go through the Narrows, or so low that it took extra time to jack off sandbars. Thus the passage through the Dells could take two or three days and a crew might make two or even three trips a season.

Raftsmen were a tough and hardy band. Pilots made several trips, often earning as much as $1,000 in a season, and carried a good deal of prestige. In the Dells, we know of three "standing pilots" who took rafts through the Dells: Louis Dupless, Robert Allen and Leroy Gates, who carved his name in the Narrows. The inscription proclaims that Gates was a "Dells and River Pilot, 1849-1858" and charged $2.00 a trip or $10.00 "if he warrants the trip."

Gates was a flamboyant character who bragged that he would pilot a raft through in his full dress suit. Many were on hand to watch and chuckle when he lost his footing and was dumped in the river.

Hiram Sly, a raft pilot, had his young son, Martin, meet him above the Narrows, boosted him on his shoulders so he wouldn't get wet when the raft was awash and gave him an unforgettable ride downstream. The Kaleas family from Kilbourn lost two brothers who drowned off rafts a year apart. Many families were understandably reluctant to allow their young sons to associate with this rough bunch of men but adventure for the boys and money for the families were strong inducements.

The sharp turn in the Narrows required expert navigation but Notch Rock was an even greater hazard. It is now entirely under water. It was a near-perfect square projection of solid rock standing out ten feet into the stream on the west bank of the Narrows slightly upstream from Rattlesnake Rock. The Rock was an even greater hazard when higher water covered it and the pilot could not see it lurking just below the surface. Again Dr. Dixon tells us, "One day in the Narrows, watching the rafts pass through, I saw a three string raft hit Notch Rock, rip off the entire right hand string of six cribs, letting the other two swing and catch on the left hand rocks, breaking in two at the middle, leaving two sections of three cribs long and two wide, with both oars unhung and the worst confusion I ever saw on a Wisconsin River raft. But the swift working lumberjacks worked the three parts together and passed on down over the dam with no serious loss of any lumber."

It takes a man to run a raft on the Wisconsin, a man who is a mixture of wildcat and alligator."

HAMLIN GARLAND

One wonders how any man could survive a raft breaking up in the Narrows. A man had to be very nimble or very lucky to run on the wet lumber. If he was thrown in the water, he might be sucked down or if he could reach the shore, how could he climb out on the irregular cliffs slippery with wet mosses?

A traveler in 1858 describes his journey to the river and the toll bridge at the Narrows which had been built in 1850 by Schuyler Gates.

Any descriptions of raftsmen and those who did business with them is likely to sound like a tale of the old Wild West. Hamlin Garland said of raftsmen, "What skill, what endurance, what courage the smallest of them displayed....Their action was titanic, their cheer superb. A day's

River drivers, "Witching up" one of the grub pins that held a lumber raft together. Early spring, when the river water was high, rough and ice cold, was the rafting season. Loggers and farmers working for extra cash, raftsmen were a tough and hardy breed. (Courtesy H.H. Bennett State Historic Site, SHSW)

labor reached from dawn to dusk, and no man thought of shirking his duty, or if he did, he was shamed into action by his fellows who took a savage pride in long hours and fatigue....On Sundays or during the long evenings they joined in contests of strength or skill. You would think they would require rest, but no! They wrestled, jumped, chinned a bar, pulled sticks, tried out each other s grip, and in every conceivable way established athletic rank....It takes a man to run a raft on the Wisconsin, a man who is a mixture of wildcat and alligator."

When the raftsmen had time or opportunity to stop and refresh themselves, these red shirts were, as Steward Edward White tells in his book, The Riverman, were "bubbling over with the joy of life, ready for quarrel if quarrel also spelled fun, drinking deep and heavy-handed and fearless in their cups."

THE WORKING RIVER   17

18 "The Dells"

The Dell House was the first inn below Pointe Basse in the 75 mile stretch from that point to Portage. After the dangers of the Dells passage were behind them, the pleasures of the Dell House were more than welcome. H.H. Bennett says that the raftsmen would, "on landing safely at the Dell House, partake freely of the concentrated river water kept there for emergencies; if the trip had not been successful and the raft had been broke up, then something must be taken to the success of the next trip; if one of the crew had been lost in the mad waters, partaking of something in token of good wishes for his hereafter was not to be neglected by any means and sometimes like token was deemed necessary for the welfare of each of his surviving relatives, and so the old place became the scene of many a boisterous time, which may be all the foundation there is for the stories of the horrible crimes committed in and about the place in the early days."

After Kilbourn was established in 1856, raftsmen also visited, sometimes to the dismay of the residents. It was said that the first thing the raftsmen did was to tie up the town marshall "so he wouldn't get hurt." Then they would head for "Bloody Run," with its many saloons and other dubious attractions. There is still speculation as to whether Bloody Run was Eddy St. or the 700 block of Superior St. south of Broadway. The lumber companies did not pay their raftsmen until the end of the trip but if the stories are true the rivermen had plenty of money to spend when they hit town.

Stewart Edward White tells of some of the raftsmen's perils. "The proprietors of these places were a bold and unscrupulous lot. In their everyday business they had to deal with the most dangerous rough-and-tumble fighters this country has ever known....Men got rich very quickly at this business. And there existed this great advantage in favor of the divekeeper: nobody cared what happened to a riverman. You could pound him over the head with a lead pipe, or drug his drink, or choke him into insensibility or rob him and throw him out into the street. The only fly in the divekeeper's ointment was that the riverman would fight back. And fight back he did....In his own words, he was a hard man to nick ."

In addition to drinking and brawling, there were other diversions. One Madam built a house on the cliffs on the right hand bank of the Lower Dells below the dam. She had her girls swing out over the river to tempt their potential customers below and then supplied "a ring in the rocks for the boys" to tie up their rafts.

Local people benefited from the lumber trade when they found free lumber floating in the river after a raft was broken up and not retrieved promptly. This practice was called river pirating and was legal if the rivermen made no claim to their lost product within a given time. The Lower Dells dock area became known as Pirate's Eddy. It is said that many houses throughout the area and in other communities up and down the river were built from this lumber.

As railroads gradually extended through the state, they replaced the lumber raft. The necessity of drilling holes for the grub pins wasted considerable lumber, some was damaged by water and some when rafts split up. Many lives were lost also. Freight was quite cheap and soon the inexhaustible forests were stripped of their virgin pine.

Rafting through the Narrows at the Dells, where the river was so deep and narrow it ran "on edge." (Courtesy H.H. Bennett State Historic Site, SHSW)

Previous page: "We were fairly afloat on the fierce, rolling, rushing tide, speeding on or rather down toward the turn above the bridge, where projecting into the stream is the dangerous rock, on the starboard hand of the river, called Notch Rock." (Courtesy H.H. Bennett State Historic Site, SHSW)

In 1890, the last raft floated down the Wisconsin and its lumber was sold to the Drinker Mills in Happy Hollow, Kilbourn. Another chapter in the history of the Wisconsin frontier had closed.

Intrigue, Conflict and Violence

"Without doubt," wrote Rick Durbin, "no dam in the state has ever had the intrigue, bitter contention, violence and financial misdeeds connected with it over such a long period as has the Kilbourn Dam on the Wisconsin River in Wisconsin Dells. Born of intrigue in 1853, it was known for a number of years as the most dangerous dam on the river. Conflicts between its developers were many, finding their way into the legislature in the late 1850 s and to the courts as well during the next several decades. Between the lumbermen's efforts and the river's periodic flooding, the dam underwent a series of modifications and reconstructions that lasted until 1897. The final chapter came with the building of the present dam at the beginning of this century when hydromania was sweeping the state. Each phase of the story is replete with its own compelling elements: scoundrels, powerful antagonists, bunglers, unique problems, battles legal, physical and otherwise and much more. Its constructions were as much a tale of man against man as they were against nature."

The construction of the first Dells dam was intimately connected with the plans of Joseph Bailey, Jonathan Bowman and other promoters of Newport; with the dubious financial schemes of Garret Vliet and Byron Kilbourn of the La Crosse and Milwaukee Railroad; and the boosterism of Alanson Holly, newspaperman and investor in Kilbourn City. The dam was the plum in the pudding and he who possessed the state charter to build the dam decided the fate of the city to be built on the river. Ultimately, the decision was made by Vliet and Kilbourn, with the perhaps unwitting cooperation of Bailey and Bowman, who transferred the charter for the Newport dam to the railroaders.

In short, when Vliet and Kilbourn were unable to strike a favorable deal on the location of the dam with riverfront landowners in Newport, they did what was necessary to build it elsewhere and elsewhere happened to be the village now known as Wisconsin Dells.

In March 1855, Vliet, Kilbourn, Bailey, Bowman, and their partners persuaded the legislature to charter the Wisconsin River Hydraulic Company for the purpose of building a dam upriver from Newport.

Work began on this first Dells dam in October 1855 under the supervision of John Anderson and Joseph Bailey. The river was 350 feet wide at the point selected with about two-thirds of it deeper than 15 feet even at low water. Constructing a dam here would be a formidable task for men working with a steam railroad, draft animals and hand tools.

In January 1858, the Hydraulic Company hired Joseph Bailey to complete the dam by the end of the year. He began by constructing a network of ten-foot-square cribs made of interlocked logs, 80 feet wide and 160 feet long, and filled with rock. Once filled, the cribs were decked over with heavy planks.

The rest of the channel was then filled with trees sunk butt-first at an angle and facing downstream, so the force of the river would drive them more solidly into the bottom. This kind of "tree-dam" was a proven and commonly-used engineering design. The trees were held in place with cross beams and stones.

The dam also had a 25-feet wide flume down which water to power a mill was directed. By law, the dam also had to have a chute or slide, 60-feet wide, to allow lumber rafts to pass down the 8-foot drop without damage. At 160 feet, the longest on the river, the Dells slide was intended to make up for the hazard the dam created. After running the Narrows and the rapids immediately downstream, the river men would now have to steer their rafts to hit the chute perfectly or break up. As experience would show, even when they hit the chute perfectly, rafts often fell off the side or broke apart in the eddy at its bottom.

The prevailing, and correct, opinion in the upstream lumber industry was "that the dam will be ruinous to the lumbering interests on the Wisconsin river..trouble will yet grow out of this dam business."

On the day Editor Holly proclaimed of the dam that, "No man who has had any knowledge of its construction has the least fear of its ever going out," a substantial portion of the crib and tree work on the east bank washed out. Repairs were made and the dam was completed in time for the rafting season of spring, 1859.

The first rafts were scheduled to pass over the dam in the afternoon of March 18. A crowd of over 100 Kilbournites lined the banks to watch. As Durbin tells the story:

"In the lead was Patrick O'Hare of Kilbourn City, who leaped and shouted and cheered as he was going over.

But his antics might have resulted more from fear than from joy. The rafts were stove to pieces and three men lost their lives...In the following weeks the dam continued to take a fearsome toll of the lumber rafts. Included were two small German children, who in a skiff accidentally cast adrift, drifted over the dam, precipitating the children into the water and drowning them."

After meeting at Kilbourn and watching a few rafts attempt to negotiate the dam, the lumbermen promised "out it will come if men, money and powder can accomplish it." A gang of raftsmen set out to tear up the dam, but were deterred by the Columbia county sheriff. A barrel of powder was planted to blast the dam, but it got wet and failed to ignite. A lawsuit succeeded where violence failed. A Columbia County jury found the dam to be a nuisance and ordered the Company to lower its height and improve the slide. Since no one, who had once promised to do so would pay for the work, it was not performed.

Finally, the lumberman tore three feet off the top of the dam, but so exposed the cribs and trees beneath that the dam now collected every bit of debris that flowed downstream. As one

The steamer Germania beached for repairs, with the Dells dam and Munger's grist mill in the background.
(Courtesy H.H. Bennett State Historic Site, SHSW)

THE WORKING RIVER   21

Construction of the hydropower dam at the Dells in 1909 resulted in higher water levels upstream. Channels were altered and islands flooded over.
(Courtesy H.H. Bennett State Historic Site, SHSW)

newspaper reported, "not a raft can pass without getting broken up."

Finally, in the fall of 1859, lumbermen and townspeople lowered the dam and the chute to about four feet in height. Still not satisfied, the lumbermen started to raise money to "take out said dam, with force either physical or legal." On the legal front the lumbermen petitioned the legislature to repeal the charter of the Hydraulic Company. On the physical front, lumberman Francis Biron, whose mill was at the head of the rapids at what is now Wisconsin Rapids, came down to the Dells with a crew to dismantle the dam. The Hydraulic Company, now bankrupt, could not stop either threat and in March 1860, the first Wisconsin Dells dam lost its legislative charter and was demolished.

During the course of the work, one of Biron's loggers fell in the river and drowned. As the story was told 50 years later, fueled by a barrel of whiskey, the loggers then stormed up to Kilbourn and threatened to burn down the village. They would have done so were they were not turned back by a pistol-toting Joseph Bailey.

The first Dells dam was a poorly-engineered, poorly-sited project, financed and run by a Company whose managers seemed to be pathologically corrupt. Their interest seemed to be less in building a solid dam that would act as a powerplant and magnet for industry and more in speculating in village lots sold at inflated prices.

In the words of one Milwaukee visitor at the time, "the tearing out of the great dam...has to a considerable extent damned the place."

It may have appeared that way in 1860, but in fact, the Dells dam gave birth to the village. The dam brought the railroad and the railroad made Kilbourn City a regional shipping center and farm market town.

So, despite the folly, chicanery and disaster that accompanied its short life, the first dam was successful in giving birth to Wisconsin Dells.

The Wisconsin River Hydraulic Company ceased to exist in January 1862 when only one director showed up for the board meeting. "No quorum," stated the minute book. There were also no funds in the treasury and no dam in the river.

As the Company's largest creditor, Byron Kilbourn then acquired the dam site and formed a new company whose board of directors was made up mainly of local people, most notably Jonathan Bowman. He submitted proposals to the legislature to create first the Columbia and later the Kilbourn Manufacturing Company which would build a three-foot high dam at the Dells.

After the debris from the Kilbourn railroad bridge, which had burned and collapsed into the river in May 1866, was cleared away, work began on the second Dells dam. It was a low dam, with a fall of two-three feet. Nonetheless, the dam was still a life-threatening hazard to raftsmen and created a loss for the lumber companies of as much as 5% of the lumber shipped on the river, the equivalent of $100,000. Litigation, legislation and recriminations came downriver throughout the rest of the 1860s, yet the courts upheld the dam's right to exist.

Byron Kilbourn died in 1870. He left his Dells interests to his son Byron H., who incorporated the Kilbourn City Flouring Mills to actually utilize the waterpower which the dam was built to create.

A mill was built on the east side and opened with a grand ceremony on February 22, 1871. "Flow on mighty river," said one speaker. "No cobwebs shall bind thee." The new mill had its work cut out for it. Before it ground its first sack of flour, it already owed $75,000 in dam building costs.

Litigation continued, but at least the mill wheels were turning. In October 1872, the mill handled 53 thousand bushels of wheat. However, the burden of lawsuits and debts became too great for Byron H. Kilbourn, who washed his hands of the dam operation that had been conceived by his father.

Further weakened by the financial depression of the mid-1870s, and unable to pay court-ordered damages to the lumbermen, the owners of the mill were forced to sell out. The buyer was one of the dam's oldest and most bitter foes, lumberman John T. Kingston of Necedah. While in Kingston's hands in 1874, the mill was destroyed by a fire probably set by rivermen, who also dismantled much of the dam.

While the rivermen battled the Dells dam, railroads laid track up the Wisconsin Valley. By the end of the 1870s, railcars would all but replace river rafts as the means to move lumber to market and the prospects rose for another Dells dam. In 1883, Ellis Munger repaired the old dam once again and reconstructed the mill. The lumbermen did not harass him but the river did, sending down a flood in the fall of 1889 that washed out his dam.

"Hydromania"

As the 19th Century turned into the 20th, a new industry came to the Wisconsin River Valley. The river that had carried logs and lumber rafts, powered sawmills and grain mills, was transformed into a generator of electrical power. Starting in 1886 and ending with the completion of the Prairie du Sac dam in 1914, the river was gripped by what one historian called "hydromania." More than twenty hydroelectric power stations were built in these years, including one at the Dells. Thus between 1859 and 1905, there was a working dam in place only 11 plus years over that 47 year period.

The Dells hydroelectric dam and power plant began when Phillip Spooner, Magnus Swenson and P. M. Porter organized the Southern Wisconsin Power Company and acquired the mill property and water power rights at Kilbourn City. To generate as much power as possible, the company proposed building a dam 17 feet high that would flood the free-running rapids and keep water levels higher than ever in the Upper Dells.

The Wisconsin Dells hydropower dam was the fifth attempt by engineers to tame the river and the first successful one.
(Courtesy H.H. Bennett State Historic Site, SHSW)

Like other dam builders at the Dells, Southern Wisconsin Power faced opposition, but not from lumbermen. Some opposition came from steamboat owner Nat Wetzel who proposed that the new dam be built with a lock so boats could pass through. The old question of navigability arose here and was ultimately resolved by building the dam without a lock. A similar question arose when the Prairie du Sac dam was built a few years later and a lock was built there, but it has never been opened for commercial traffic.

Compensation for upriver landowners whose property would be flooded was also a question, and one reminiscent of the Newport conflict. Now it was settled simply, when the power company agreed to pay Wetzel and the Dells Company for flooding their property.

The leading, and practically the only, person to oppose the dam was H. H. Bennett. However, as he said, "very few of my good Kilbourn neighbors feel this way and most of them believe now that the Dells will be quite as beautiful with fifteen feet of them under water." The promise of jobs, industry, growth and Progress that dams at the Dells had always extended but had yet to deliver was too strong to resist.

Bennett's dream of preserving the Dells was overwhelmed by that of a man of equal earnestness and dedication, Magnus Swenson. A successful industrialist who made his fortune as a sugar beet processor, Swenson was one of the founders of the Southern Wisconsin Power Company and a full convert to hydromania. He hired a young Madison engineer named Daniel Mead to design a dam that would survive in the difficult conditions at the Dells.

Workers used picks, shovels and explosives to excavate a foundation in the riverbed sandstone. Some 165,000 yards of material were transported from the site by horse and wagon. The base of the dam was constructed of hewn wooden cribs matched to the contour of the river's rock bottom, floated into place and sunk under the weight of rockfill. Steam engines drove pumps to dewater cofferdams and served to power a concrete mixer, but all the concrete in the dam's base and superstructure was delivered to the forms by wheelbarrow.

Although all available local men were employed on the job, more workers were needed. As many as 400 laborers, many immigrants from Bulgaria and Austria, were hired in Chicago and Milwaukee. Wages were $2.00 a day for laborers, while a man and his team could earn $4.00. Work began in December 1906 and the first power was generated in August, 1909.

The dam they built is 340 feet long, and raises the Wisconsin River 17 feet at its base. Generating capacity of the plant is 8,200 kilowatts, or 10,992 horsepower. Installed generating equipment consists of three 2,000-KW and one 2,200-KW generators. Originally, the plant generated at 25 cycles, but later was converted to 60 cycles.

During the course of construction, another problem arose. Located where the municipal dock was later built, the village waterworks would surely be flooded out by the new dam. In 1906, the power company promised to compensate the city for its loss by providing 1,000 kW a day, free, for all time.

Unlike its predecessors, the Kilbourn hydro dam was a successful example of engineering and construction expertise. However, when it came to finances, the Southern Wisconsin Power

Company had much in common with earlier Dells dam builders. In his enthusiasm to build first the Dells dam, and soon after, the dam at Prairie du Sac, Swenson apparently did not pay close enough attention to where he was going to sell the power his station generated.

It was assumed that electric railway companies in Milwaukee and its western suburbs would purchase the power at a profitable rate. Indeed, some of the first power generated at the Dells went to run trolleys in Watertown, but the railway lines all owned by Milwaukee's electric company agreed to pay no more for Dells electricity than the cost of producing it. This financially ruinous arrangement remained in force until the late 1920s, even after Wisconsin Power & Light purchased the station.

Another market for Dells electric power might have been the industrial development that dam promoters claimed would come to the village. During construction, many perspective factory owners visited the town representing companies making everything from canvas gloves to pianos. Some were even offered free land near the plant, none stayed.

No matter how ill the wind, it usually blows fairly for someone and, in the case of the finances of the Dells hydropower plants, farmers benefitted. With more power than it could sell profitably, the utility ran lines through rural Sauk and Columbia that made farmers there among the first in Wisconsin to have electricity. After it became part of the Wisconsin Power and Light Company, the Dells station helped to link Reedsburg, Baraboo, Sauk City, Spring Green and other small communities in the region into one of the state's first interconnected utility systems.

In 1924, several southern and central Wisconsin utilities were united under the name Wisconsin Power and Light Company. It now supplies electric service in 33 Wisconsin counties, serving roughly one-third of Wisconsin, and including service to 386 communities and 39,000 rural customers.

The hydropower dam, the fifth dam at Kilbourn, still stands with modifications, repairs and upgrading made over the years. Today it can produce a maximum of 10,000 KW, enough to supply 10,000 homes. The average production over a year is 6,000 KW depending on the river level.

From the river-rafting days to the hydropower era, the old saying, "it's water over the dam" has always had special significance at Wisconsin Dells.

The Great Flood of 1938

When high water hits the Wisconsin River, as it did in June of 1993 at 18.6 feet, comparisons are made to floods of the past. On September 14, 1938, the Wisconsin River reached a record-breaking 23.8 feet. The Wisconsin Dells Events of September 15, 1938, reported. "East of this city in the town of Lewiston some of the lowland has been covered by the flood waters and some damage was done.

Tuesday morning the river had risen sufficiently to flood parts of highway 13 north of this city so that a detour was established.

No boats were run up river on Tuesday and the tourist business was at a standstill. The municipal dock broke from its mooring about eleven o clock Tuesday evening and the fire company, augmented by a large number of citizens turned out to the rescue."

According to the report from the local power plant, the water in the Wisconsin River reached a height of 15.8, which is the highest that has ever been recorded since the plant was installed here. All of the gates in the dam were open and the water carrying much debris in the shape of logs, roots and trees was a never ending sight.

People came from far distant points to line the river bank and hundreds of cars lined the banks of the river at times to see the torrent as it passed.

The boiling, churning, swirling waters of the Narrows could be heard roaring as far away as River Road. Giant s Shield above Cold Water Canyon and Leroy Gates name in the Narrows were covered. Upstream, Highway 13 flooded over at Plainville and the Stand Rock Road was closed to traffic.

One foot of water covered Highway 12 and the Lower Dells boat docks were flooded. People watching the water roar over the dam were shocked when they saw a team of horses drowned and still in their harnesses floating down the swollen river.

The floods of 1993 in Missouri, Iowa and North Dakota were shocking and memorable, but in the Wisconsin Dells, the flood of 1938 was the high water to remember.

FOUR
THE RAILROAD MAKES A CITY

Great Promise and Bitter Disappointment

There is no guillotine in this "tale of two cities," and few of its details resemble the romantic and intriguing novel of Charles Dickens. This tale does, however, speak of greed, conspiracy, wealth, poverty, the birth of one city and the death of another.

The tale begins in the newly-settled area on the east and west banks of the Wisconsin River, about two miles south of the present city of Wisconsin Dells.

In November, 1852, apparently at the suggestion of Joseph Bailey and Jonathan Bowman, the Columbia County Board named the new town Newport. Bailey and Bowman had just completed a warehouse on the river and they hoped that a place named "Newport" would attract steamboat traffic.

Joseph Bailey had already become one of the leading characters in the tale by making a claim, in 1850, to a large section of land in Newport located along the east bank of the Wisconsin River. He had also, along with partner John Marshall, obtained a charter from the state legislature to construct a bridge across the Wisconsin at the mouth of Dell Creek.

In 1851, Jonathon Bowman, a wealthy young attorney, recently graduated from law school, and Dr. George Jenkins, a graduate of the University of New York medical college, also arrived at Newport. Together with Bailey they agreed that Newport would be an ideal spot for a thriving new town and they began to work toward that end. Joseph Kendrick, John Steele and Marshall, who had located on the west side of the river, agreed that they also would work toward development of a new village.

The developers felt the river would offer power for "all the mills that could be erected on its banks." They also knew that the railroad then under construction from Milwaukee to La Crosse had to cross the Wisconsin somewhere between Portage and Point Bluff and they figured that Newport would be the best place for it.

In 1853, in addition to the charter for a bridge they already had, Bowman, Bailey and several others obtained a legislative charter to build a dam across the river.

At the same time their group was making overtures to Byron Kilbourn, newly elected president of the La Crosse and Milwaukee Railroad, to secure his promise to cross the river at Newport.

The next step for Bowman and Bailey was to plat 400 acres of land which they owned into marketable lots in the new village of Newport. The lots began selling immediately at very high prices. The village grew quickly. By the summer of 1854 many homes and businesses were constructed. By 1855, about 1500 people resided in the blossoming young village which contained 13 large stores, three hotels and other businesses.

E.C. Dixon in his "Newport, Its Rise and Fall" wrote, "Not many communities in the United States were founded with a greater promise of permanent well-being...few faded so suddenly or left behind more bitter disappointment."

According to the history of Columbia County, "As a further inducement to secure the crossing of the railroad in Newport, Bailey and Bowman agreed to make a transfer of their 400 acres and their charter for the dam to Byron Kilbourn. In return, he offered bonds worth $200,000 to insure his promise to build the dam and to cross the river at Newport."

Garret Vliet, vice-president of the La Crosse and Milwaukee, was Byron Kilbourn's repre-

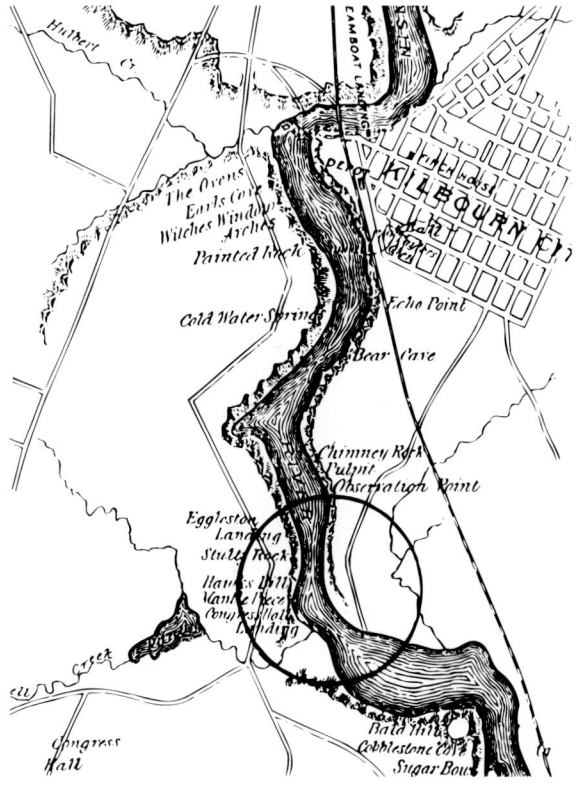

The circle indicates the bend in the river up from the mouth of Dell Creek where the grand city of Newport was to be located. The dotted line is the route of the railroad that bypassed Newport and gave birth to Kilbourn/Wisconsin Dells.

Previous page: The Kilbourn State Bank and Stuelke's Drugs on the corner of Broadway and Superior in the 1910s.
(Courtesy H.H. Bennett State Historic Site, SHSW)

THE RAILROAD MAKES A CITY 27

Dixon's Canada Store was the grandest general store in early Kilbourn. It was destroyed by fire in 1866. (Courtesy H.H. Bennett State Historic Site, SHSW)

sentative at Newport. After the deal was made with Kilbourn, Vliet, along with Bailey and Bowman, completed platting the remainder of the 400 acres.

When the people of Newport found out about the additional land development, lots were grabbed up quickly. It was said that some parties were able to double their money in 24 hours time.

At the same time that the flourish of activity was taking place east of the river the land owners on the other side of the river were busy laying out a village they called Dell Creek. The name Dell Creek was later dropped to become part of the larger village of Newport. The entire area of Newport, east and west of the river, was originally platted for a population of 10,000.

Shortly after a weak attempt to begin construction of the promised dam, Vliet, acting for Kilbourn, and on behalf of the developers, proposed the organization of a corporation, which came to be known as the Wisconsin River Hydraulic Company. The stated purpose of the corporation was to avoid individual responsibility from damage which might result from flooding upstream when the new dam was completed.

Vliet then conveyed to the new company the real estate secured from Bailey and Bowman and the charter for the building of the dam as well as the bonds given to Bailey and Bowman and their partners.

Owners of land likely to be flooded when the dam went in openly discussed the high sums they were going to demand in damages. These threats alarmed the directors of the Hydraulic Company, who feared that their profits would be eroded. Using this as a stated rationale, they asked that the $200,000 in bonds be returned to Kilbourn. Bailey, Bowman and the incorporators of the dam had faith that the Hydraulic Company would fulfill its pledge to build the dam and that the railroad would keep its pledge to cross the river at Newport.

Their faith, it seems, was misplaced. While assuring the people of their intentions to fulfill their part of the bargain, the Hydraulic Company was busy buying land two miles up river, at the site not yet known as Kilbourn.

In the summer of 1855, while Newport was growing rapidly, the Hydraulic Company was busy buying the entire tract of land on which Kilbourn was located. Knowledge of the purchase caused a near panic but the railroad company still gave assurances that the promise of a bridge at Newport would be fulfilled.

It did not happen. When the railroad was built north from Portage in 1857, the tracks bypassed Newport and crossed the river at the Hydraulic Company's site named in honor of Byron Kilbourn. The city that became Wisconsin Dells was born and the boom town of Newport became a ghost village marked by the memory of shattered dreams.

Byron Kilbourn
(Courtesy, New Past Press, Inc.)

Byron Kilbourn

As President of the La Crosse and Milwaukee Railroad in the 1850s, Byron Kilbourn was responsible for the siting of the village that became Wisconsin Dells. Although originally named in his honor, Kilbourn City actually saw very little of Byron Kilbourn. It was never his home, only a potentially good investment.

Byron Kilbourn was born at Granby, Connecticut, on Sept. 8, 1801. In 1802 his father bought 16,000 acres of land in central Ohio, around Columbus, and the next year moved there with his family.

The law had been young Byron's favorite subject, but his father's strong prejudice against that profession changed the son's mind. Byron had always enjoyed the outdoors, so he coupled his interest with his mathematical training and went into surveying.

Ohio was then laying out vast internal improvements, and the young Kilbourn became an engineer on several of the projects, including the Ohio river canal, the Miami canal and the Milan ship canal. These completed, he set out for "that far off country to the west of Lake Michigan" and got a job as surveyor of public lands at Green Bay in May, 1834.

The surveying job was merely a way station for the ambitious Kilbourn. He spent most of the summer and fall of 1834 exploring the western shore of the lake, seeking "the natural commercial point."

From the moment he first looked west across the Milwaukee river from Solomon Juneau's place, he knew he had found the site for his city. The land was too swampy, and the bluffs were too steep for building sites, but these difficulties were just a challenge to the young engineer.

"If we build the first [Railroad] and get to the river first, Chicago will not dare to approach our territory. Then we can defy the world to come between us and this great northwest."
—BYRON KILBOURN

He moved his family to Milwaukee from Cincinnati in September, 1837, and built a log house in what is now Lapham Park. He lived in this city until his death, August 5, 1877, supporting many projects for civic improvement. Except for two terms as mayor, he avoided public office.

Kilbourn was to have his fling at railroads, but not until after he tried canal-building. The canal was to run from the Milwaukee River to the Menomonee River then cut west to the Rock River and on to the four lakes of the Madison area, the Wisconsin River and thence to the Mississippi.

The Milwaukee Road's diesel-electric, high-speed streamliner Hiawatha roared over the Wisconsin Dells bridge in the 1940s.
(Courtesy H.H. Bennett State Historic Site, SHSW)

Kilbourn pushed this Milwaukee and Rock River canal by every means, even founding the city's first newspaper, the Milwaukee Advertiser, in July, 1836, to promote it. In 1838 Kilbourn won a temporary victory when Congress granted 166,400 acres of land to be sold to finance construction and the legislature gave the company a charter. The first dirt was dug from the canal bed on the Fourth of July, 1839, and the dam and portion of the canal running parallel to the Milwaukee river was opened in 1842. That same year, however, the project's enemies persuaded the legislature to repeal the acts which would have permitted the canal's completion. Even so, there was enough canal to give water power for "75 run of millstones." Soon 24 flour mills, lumber mills and factories—Milwaukee's first industrial district—were humming busily on its banks. Although the canal was never finished, Byron Kilbourn was not discouraged. He was already thinking about railroads.

Kilbourn particularly wanted his young city of Milwaukee to beat its rival Chicago in building a railroad to the Mississippi. He said, "If we build the first one and get to the river first,

Chicago will not dare to approach our territory. Then we can defy the world to come between us and this great northwest."

In 1847, the state legislature chartered the Milwaukee & Waukesha railroad. Kilbourn, who was elected mayor of Milwaukee in 1848, became president of the new railroad company. Next the legislature amended the charter to allow the railroad to extend its lines to the Mississippi, and the company changed its name to the Milwaukee & Mississippi Railroad Company. Construction of the Milwaukee to Waukesha portion of the line began in 1849.

Kilbourn's company didn't have enough money to buy rails for this short distance, for Milwaukee investors at that time considered toll roads surfaced with planks a better investment. Money was so scarce that the railroad even accepted stock subscriptions in commodities. For the first year the grading was paid for almost entirely in orders for goods: "by carts from wagon makers, by harness from harness makers, and by cattle, horses, beef, pork, oats, corn, potatoes, and flour from the farmers," as one of the first directors, Edward D. Holton, recalled in an address in 1858.

The first trip all the way to Waukesha was made in February, 1851. Passengers even helped the train crew stack wood that first year before taking their seats.

Kilbourn's ambition was not satisfied with this first section of the railroad, and the work was pushed vigorously in the next few years. Farmers along the route loaned the railroad workers teams and implements, and often pitched in and helped without pay. The road pushed on to Milton in 1852, to Stoughton in 1853, to Madison in 1854, and to Prairie du Chien, on the Mississippi, on April 15, 1857.

Kilbourn was not through with railroads. He became a commissioner of the Milwaukee & Watertown railroad, then president of the La Crosse railroad, both of which were later absorbed by the Milwaukee Road.

It was in the La Crosse venture that Kilbourn ran off the track of civic rectitude and got mired in a lobbying scandal of greater magnitude than any other legislative corruption ever uncovered in Wisconsin.

In the 1980s, community organizations and individuals raised the money and supplied labor to build a new depot at the Dells in the style of the original station built a century earlier. (Courtesy H.H. Bennett State Historic Site, SHSW)

In 1856, while the La Crosse railroad was still under construction, Congress authorized two large grants of land in Wisconsin for railroad purposes. The state legislature was empowered to assign the grants to railroads. One grant, in eastern Wisconsin, went to the Wisconsin and Superior Co., later absorbed by the North Western railroad, and the other went to Kilbourn's La Crosse railroad.

A legislative investigating committee was created in 1858 to look into charges that bribery had been used to get the La Crosse grant. The committee made some very shocking discoveries, which were published in a "Wisconsin Black Book" that year.

The report said that railroad officials, headed, by Kilbourn, had paid more than $1,000,000 in bonds and stocks for "expenses incident to the land grant."

Of this amount, $631,000 was paid in bribes to a majority of the legislature, the governor and a supreme court justice, the book said. The rest of the stocks and bonds went to compensate the lobbyists who had swarmed like bees around the capitol while Kilbourn's grant was pending.

The standard price paid to bribe an assemblyman was $5,000, the report stated, but state senators cost twice as much. "Key men" and those who helped line up their colleagues were even more liberally "remembered," three senators getting $20,000 each and one $25,000.

Governor Coles L. Bashford, Wisconsin's first Republican governor, received $50,000, the report showed, and Supreme Court Justice Abram D. Smith "found $10,000 in bonds in his library desk in Milwaukee" - and put them in his safe deposit box.

Some of the legislators could not be bought. Senator Amassa Cobb of Mineral Point reported this interview with a Kilbourn agent:

> "I asked him what was the amount of the capital stock of the company. He replied, $10,000,000. I told him to say to Byron Kilbourn that if he would multiply the capital stock by the number of leaves in Capitol park and give me the amount of money, and then have himself, Moses Strong and Alex Mitchell blacked and give me a clear title to them as servants for life, I would take the matter under consideration."

Milwaukee was strangely lenient with Kilbourn after this scandalous expose. He had done so much in the building of the city that it seems he could do no wrong in the eyes of Milwaukeeans.

His company went into liquidation soon after the scandal, but Kilbourn was left by no means a poor man. He lived in Milwaukee like a respectable citizen until the fall of 1868, when poor health led him to travel south. He died in Jacksonville, Florida, December 16, 1870.

FIVE
The Civil War

Heroes Off To War

On April 15, 1861, President Abraham Lincoln issued a call to the states to provide 75,000 militia men to suppress the rebellion in the southern states. Wisconsin's quota was relatively small, with only one regiment of 780 men requested. By the end of the year, after hostilities had actually begun, the state's levy had risen to 19 regiments of infantry, four regiments of cavalry and five artillery companies. Among these first units to muster for service was the 12th Wisconsin Infantry and the 4th Wisconsin Cavalry, both with men from the Wisconsin Dells area.

Company E of the 12 Wisconsin Infantry was formed at Delton, and its history was recorded by one of its men, Hosea Rood. The following is an edited excerpt of the Company's journey from Delton to Madison on its way to active duty.

"And so it was one morning made known to us that on the 31st day of October we were to take our departure for Camp Randall, Madison, where companies like ours from various parts of the state were being organized into regiments, and where the regiments thus formed were being properly officered and drilled for active service in the field.

"Here were a hundred men and boys who had, from the conviction of duty to their beloved country, sworn to leave homes, families and friends, and give themselves to the service of their country in her time of need...

"And so, though some tears were shed, they were not the bitter tears of regret. They were tears that in an unguarded moment forced themselves to the surface from the depths of emotion that throbbed in the loving, loyal hearts of both those who were to go and those who were to stay.

"But, hark! there is Trume Hurlburt's drum? He is beating the call to fall in. The boys gather promptly in front of Newman's Tavern, and at Captain Vanderpoel's order form in line for the last time in Delton.

"The brief partings over, all by common consent stand back, except two or three mothers and wives who cannot seem to find the last word. But the old Captain draws his sword, gives the order, Right face! Forward, counter-march by file left, March! and the men are on the move. They march down around by Topping's store, and then file left, and there drawn up in order on the road between the store and The Gully, are thirteen farm teams, and these are to take us to Madison. As the company marches alongside the wagons, eight men climb into each. In a minute all are loaded, and the procession moves forward. After crossing "The Gully" and coming up in front of the old red blacksmith shop on the left, the team in front stops, and the others draw up in close order around a wagon in the center, in which stands with uncovered head, Mr. Green, the village preacher. It has not seemed fitting to send forth our Company without public prayer to the God of battles in our behalf; and so this good man, whose life work it is to stand between the living and the dead and point the way to brighter worlds beyond this one, stands ready now to commend us to the care of Him who watches with like tenderness over country, Home and Heaven.

The prayer ended, the team in front moves forward again, the others following in order while the gathered people, not to lose sight of their departing soldier-boys, walk alongside the wagons as they move slowly toward the bridge across Dell Creek, at the lower end of the village..."Yes, that was a jolly ride, though it was not all a ride. The rough boards laid across the wagon boxes for seats had been put by some mistake or other with their hard sides up; and before we got well across Webster Prairie they proved rather tiresome to the anatomy. Before we came to Baraboo, Charley Briggs, Laredo Smith, Henry Marston, George Lawsha, Ed Bennett, and a dozen others, took to their heels, in order to rest themselves, and, at the same time, cultivate an acquaintance with those who dwelt by the wayside.

> *"Here were a hundred men and boys who had...sworn to leave homes, families and friends...."*
> —Hosea Rood

Previous page:
Young Henry H. Bennett ready to march to war and his sister Sarah.
(Courtesy H.H. Bennett State Historic Site, SHSW)

The once-merry boys of Company E who marched gladly off to war in 1861, gathered for a reunion in 1900. ((Courtesy H.H. Bennett State Historic Site, SHSW)

"The good people of Baraboo had heard of our coming, and had got out their little Fourth of July cannon, and as we rode down through their streets, they made the welcome ring with as much of war noise as they were able.

"They hung out their flags, waved their handkerchiefs, and hurrahed till they were hoarse, and we appreciated it all in having no small opinion of both them and ourselves. Altogether, our passage through the thriving little town was a pleasant thing to remember-enough so to make the writer cherish kindly recollections of the place.

"We crossed the Wisconsin river at what was then known as "Matt's Ferry" [Merrimac]... At dark we reached the village of Lodi, twenty miles from Madison, where supper and sleeping accommodations had been engaged for us. The occasion of keeping the company overnight was an interesting one to the patriotic people of this little village that had already sent a large number of her young men to the front. Their brass band turned out and, taking the lead of the company, paraded the principal streets of the town, and so made good friends of every one of the boys.

"Early next morning the procession of wagons was again on the road to Madison. Six miles from Lodi, as the teams wound around the hill where the old Harvey post office used to stand, the colors floating from the wagon in advance, and Truman Hurlburt, Rube Green and Jim Solomon making the attention of a young man digging potatoes on the farm of Mr. Butterfield. The great question of the day, to enlist or not to enlist, had been present in this young man's mind for several weeks, and demanding an answer; yet the answer he had been unable up to this time to settle upon. But the sight of this company of men, the flag, the music, the thoughts, That is John Gillespie's company, and I have an old school mate in that company, brought Daniel Titus to a quick decision.

" I'll do it! he said.

"The procession halted, the young man made known his desire to become one of the company, wrote his name on the roll, and then with uncovered head and uplifted hand took the oath of service. Hurrying back to the house, he changed his clothing, found in one of the wagons a seat beside his old school-mate, and then went on with his newly-made comrades to camp.

"Would Daniel Titus have done all this so eagerly had he known that the day was coming July 28, '64 when his young life would be demanded of him as a sacrifice for the bright flag floating above him that first morning in November, '61? It would have been quite like him to do so.

"About the middle of the afternoon we passed through the streets of the city of Madison and out toward Camp Randall. When near camp we left the wagons, formed into line, and with feelings alternating between soldierly pride and curiosity to see what kind of a place a military camp was, and what kind of people there were in it, we marched by the guards, through the gate, and were - in camp."

The Twelfth Wisconsin served in the western campaigns with Ulysses. S. Grant in Tennessee and at Vicksburg. Later they marched from Atlanta to the sea with William T. Sherman, and on to Washington D.C. where they took part in the Grand Review of the Union army on May 23, 1865.

"The Best Engineering Feat Ever Performed"

Although the Union forces had won great victories at Vicksburg and Gettysburg in July 1863, the Civil War dragged on indeterminably. As the war entered its fourth year in the spring of 1864, vast armies on both sides were still in the field. The Union had succeeded in dismembering the South along the Mississippi River and now hoped to carry the struggle into the fertile region west of the river.

Foreign intrigues were also afoot. In 1863, the French Emperor Napoleon III had sent a French army into Mexico to establish a puppet state under the Austrian Archduke Maximilian, who called himself the Emperor of Mexico. The United States favored the ousted republican government of Benito Juarez, who continued to struggle against the European invaders. Maximilian favored the Confederacy and, if he succeeded in Mexico, posed a threat to the Union.

The federal government determined to strike in 1864 and seize the strongholds of the Southwest. Shreveport, Louisiana, on the Red River 250 miles west of the Mississippi, was singled out for capture and occupation. A joint campaign of the army and navy would subdue the Shreveport area and move into Texas. General Nathaniel P. Banks was to move an army of 25,000 men up the Red River valley, supported by a flotilla of twenty gunboats and transports under Rear Admiral David D. Porter.

From the beginning, plans did not work smoothly. There were disagreements among Union generals; preparations were inadequate and difficulties arose in establishing a functioning civil government in Louisiana. When in readiness, the army moved parallel to the river in a column twenty miles long. Encountering no serious opposition on the advance, it would soon move far ahead of Porter's fleet, which crawled slowly in the shallow waters above Alexandria.

Then, on April 8, within fifty miles of Shreveport, there was a sudden attack. Led by General Richard Taylor, son of former U. S. President Zachary Taylor, the Confederates threw the advancing Union army into confusion. Banks had great difficulty withdrawing his infantry. After nearly two hours of sharp fighting the disorganized Union forces fell back fifteen miles with more than 3,000 men lost. It seemed that the Red River campaign was doomed to end in humiliation and disaster.

New difficulties now made the military situation alarming. Just at the time when the Red River should be overflowing its banks with the spring flood, it suddenly began to fall. Fearing that his fleet would be caught on the shoals and sandbars, Admiral Porter started to descend the stream. With the Union army deprived of this support, the Confederates attacked again and again. Slowly the Federal army retreated and by April 25 had fallen back to Alexandria.

Now an unforeseen crisis arose. Before Porter's fleet could reach the rocky channel above Alexandria, the river had "run out on him." Within that mile the Red River drops a total of thirteen feet over two distinct rapids. Perilously huge boulders nosed their heads above the surface. Nature had sprung a trap that obstructed Porter's return. Some of the army engineers suggested destroying the $2,000,000 marooned flotilla to prevent its capture by the Confederates. Even to Admiral Porter escape seemed impossible.

Joseph E. Bailey, hero of the Red River campaign. (Courtesy, Bud Gussel)

On shore was at least one soldier who thought differently. His name was Lieutenant Colonel Joseph Bailey, at first a captain in the Fourth Wisconsin Cavalry with men from the Wisconsin Dells area. Bailey had also served in the engineer corps and, as early as April 9th, saw the dilemma on the river and communicated his fears to General John Franklin, his superior officer.

Experience had taught Colonel Bailey lessons not found in books on engineering. Born in Ashtabula County, Ohio, in May, 1827, he had come to Wisconsin in 1849, participated in the founding of Newport and Kilbourn, and supervised the construction of the first Kilbourn dam.

General Franklin went to Admiral Porter with Colonel Bailey's idea. He proposed to build a dam that would raise the water level of the river upstream of the stranded gunboats. When the water level grew high enough, the dam would be pierced, and the resulting flood would float the fleet out of the shallows to safety. Bailey had seen dams like this one employed in the Wisconsin pineries where they were known as "driving dams" and used on nearly every stream to build a head of water to drive logs downstream. Although the Red was larger than a northwoods creek, Bailey was positive his "driving dam" would work.

"If damming it would get the fleet off, I would have been afloat long ago," a skeptical Admiral Porter is said to have observed.

The plan was generally condemned. Officers ridiculed it and engineers declared it impossible to

Fleeing from slavery in Tennessee, Tom Allen and his wife accompanied Company E for three years, cooking, cleaning and caring for the wounded.
(Courtesy New Past Press)

build. But Colonel Bailey persisted.

"I am convinced that it will save the fleet," urged General Franklin, the one outstanding officer who had faith in Bailey's proposal.

"The proposition looks like madness, but Colonel Bailey is so sanguine of success that I shall direct it to be tried," Admiral Porter concluded.

So on April 26, when the squadron arrived at the shoals, Admiral Porter requested General Banks to execute the plan.

"There are 3,000 idle men and 300 wagons at your disposal," General Banks told Colonel Bailey. "Now let's see what you can do."

Requesting the pinery boys from the 23rd and 29th Wisconsin regiments and the 29th Maine volunteers, all of whom were familiar with logging operations, and the 97th and 99th Colored Infantry, Bailey set the work in motion. A dam, constructed of logs, brush, brick and stone, was run out from the left bank. From the right bank cribs of stone were built. Barges were sunk near the center.

Men worked to their armpits in water under a broiling hot sun. Night and day, they labored patiently and enthusiastically. For thirty-six hours Colonel Bailey stood over the work, neither eating nor sleeping. His tall form became lank and his weight fell to 130 pounds. Eight days of incessant labor passed. Then an accident occurred to the barges and water rushed downstream. Four of the vessels escaped on this deluge of water, but the gunboats were still stranded. Undismayed, the men bent more earnestly to the task of repairs. Two wing dams were constructed up stream to lift the back water. Up, up rose the river almost to overflowing.

On May 12 the crucial moment had arrived. An estimated 30,000 people crowded the Red River banks. One long pull and the dam center collapsed. There was a tremendous rush of current. Undamaged, the marooned gunboats swept over the rocks to make their escape into deeper waters.

Colonel Bailey's plan had triumphed. The mad thunder of the released waters through the dam bore his name to immortality.

"Words are inadequate to express the admiration I feel for the ability of Lieutenant Colonel Bailey," wrote

Confederate Spy at the Dells

The Wisconsin Dells sightseeing launch "Belle Boyd" is named for the rebel spy from Martinsburg, Virginia who bravely aided Confederate Generals Stuart, Beauregard, and Jackson, and risked her life for her beloved Shenandoah Valley during the Civil War.

The most famous of Belle Boyd's spying exploits was her role in Stonewall Jackson's "Valley Campaign." Using her flirtatious charms upon a romance-smitten aide to a Union general, Belle was able to learn of a secret war council to be held in the parlor of the Front Royal Hotel. Hiding in a closet overhead, she listened through a knothole in the floor to strategy intended to take Jackson's troops by surprise. Belle returned undetected to her room and in the first hours of morning, crept to the stables, saddled her horse, and set out on a dangerous moonlight ride. Making her way past two federal sentries, she delivered her message to Colonel Turner Ashly, and was home again before sunrise. This information led to the defeat of federal troops at Port Republic and a proclamation of admiration and friendship by Jackson for the daring young Belle. He later commissioned her a captain and made her an honorary staff aide.

By the end of the war, Belle was a nationally-known figure. She spent her later years travelling the country lecturing and presenting dramatic narratives of her spying adventures. On June 9th, 1900, Belle arrived in Wisconsin Dells, scheduled to give a recital to the local G.A.R. Post. Accompanied by her third husband, Nathaniel High, she checked into room #1 of the Hile House. Two days later, at the age of 56, Isabelle Boyd High suffered a fatal heart attack. After funeral services at the local Episcopal Church, she was buried with full military honors by Wisconsin Civil War veterans.

In 1976 a memorial was completed with stone from each of the Confederate states. A historical plaque with Belle's famous post-war plea, "One God, one flag, one people - forever," was unveiled at the memorial service. Since then, twice a year, on Memorial Day and on the 4th of July, the U.S. flag, the flag of the state of Virginia and the Confederate Naval Jack fly over her grave.

It is one of history's ironies that she is buried only a short distance from former slave Tom Allen, whose heroic efforts on behalf of soldiers fighting to save the Union Belle Boyd conspired to destroy, have received less recognition.

Admiral Porter in his report to the Navy department. "This is without doubt the best engineering feat ever performed."

"Leaving out his ability as an engineer - the credit he has conferred upon the country - he has saved the Union a valuable fleet worth nearly $2,000,000; more, he has deprived the enemy of a triumph that would have emboldened them to carry on the war a year or two longer."

National approval almost overwhelmed Bailey. On June 11, 1864, Congress adopted a resolution of commendation for his "distinguished services in the recent campaign on the Red River." Bailey was one of only 15 officers of all the thousands who served in the Civil War so commended by Congress

"I get daily letters of thanks from all portions of the country," wrote the bewildered Bailey to a friend late in June.

The officers of Admiral Porter's fleet presented him with a beautiful gold mounted sword and a three gallon silver punch bowl valued at several thousand dollars. Before the war was over, on recommendations of Secretary of War Edwin M. Stanton, Colonel Bailey was promoted to the rank of brigadier general. At the end of the war he was transferred to Fort Scott, Kansas.

General Bailey found fame as elusive as the shadows. Within two years he was appealing to his old Wisconsin friend, United States Senator James Doolittle, to find him a position. Admiral Porter wrote to President Johnson requesting that General Bailey be appointed an Indian agent, either to the Chickasaws or Choctaws in Oklahoma.

"He is now suffering from wounds received in the war and also from disease contracted during that time, and thus is prevented leading his former life of civil engineer," urged Admiral Porter upon the president. Johnson could not help Bailey, who was one of thousands of decorated veterans now unemployed and petitioning him for a government position. Discouraged, Bailey removed to Nevada, Missouri and was elected sheriff of Vernon County. On March 25, 1867, while attempting to make an arrest, he was killed by two desperadoes. There he is buried.

Nearly thirty years after his death there came a pitiable sequel to Bailey's story. In want, his daughter, Ella Bailey, who remained in Missouri, appealed to the Wisconsin legislature to purchase the mementoes given to her father by Admiral Porter and his staff. An appropriation of $2,000 was rushed through the legislature and with the help of Major Guy Pierce, the golden sword and silver bowl were transferred to the State Historical Museum, Madison, where they have since been on display.

Interest in General Bailey was renewed with the news of this calamitous episode. That he might ever after be held in grateful remembrance, his portrait, with the Red River and flotilla blended into the background, was painted and hung in the governor's reception room of Wisconsin's Capitol.

Tom Allen, his wife and four children returned to the Dells and made their homes here in the 1870s.
(Courtesy H.H. Bennett State Historic Site, SHSW)

Soldiers Saddened at Death of Friend
(Taken from the *Wisconsin Mirror*, January 10, 1874)

"Died: In this village on Saturday last, Thomas Allen, aged about 40 years.

Mr. Allen had been a resident of Kilbourn about ten years. He was born in Tennessee and, until the war gave him his freedom, had been a slave. When the 12th Wisconsin was in the vicinity of Humboldt, Tennessee in 1862, Tom and [his wife] came into camp. He served the boys of this regiment faithfully two years. When the regiment came home on veteran furlough, Tom came home here with Lt. Griffin, Henry H. Bennett and others. Since then he has earned an honest livelihood for himself and family, and was universally respected by all our citizens. He was upright and truly honest. He leaves a wife and four bright little ones to mourn his loss."

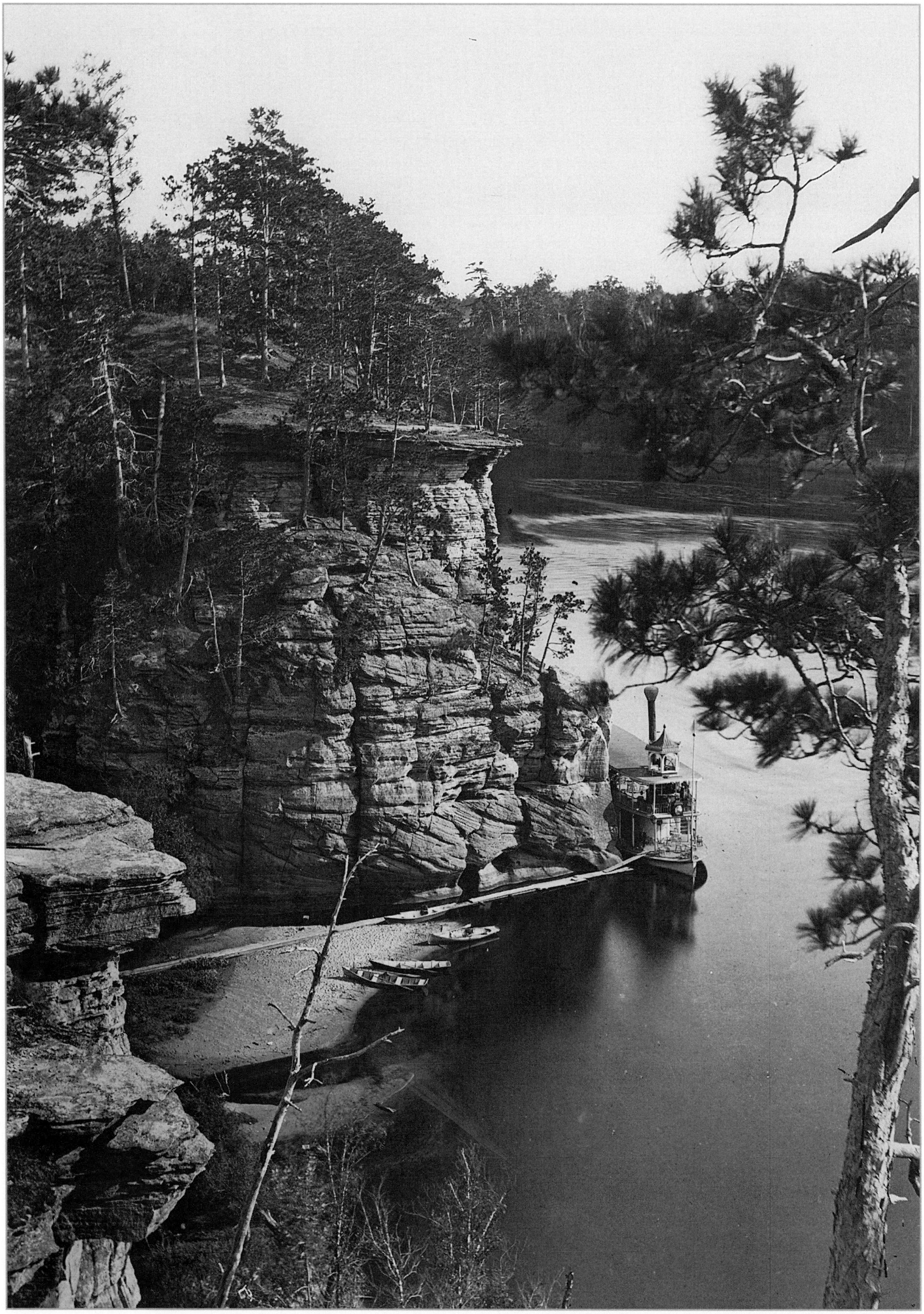

SIX
"WISCONSIN'S MOST POPULAR VACATION SPOT"

"A Place of Resort for Seekers of Pleasure"

Wisconsin Dells is one of the oldest resort areas in the state. Kilbourn was not a year old on March 25, 1856, when Wisconsin Mirror editor Alanson Holly wrote in an article that, "We conclude that the wild, romantic scenery of the Dells will always make them a place of resort for seekers of pleasure." At that time, the city consisted of eleven dwellings and one business building housing the printing office.

In the September 23rd issue of the same year, we find the following news item, "Pleasure seekers will be interested in the advertisement of Leroy Gates who is prepared to show them all the beauties and wonders of the Dells." The ad continued:

> "For Recreation Resort to the Dells! Where depressed spirits can be alleviated, gloom and melancholy soon be dispelled and the mind become Greatly invigorated. Leroy Gates has purchased a pleasure Boat for the purpose of penetrating the numerous occult caves of the Dells."

This surely was a rowboat and there is nothing to show how many passengers were shown through those "occult caves" by Mr. Gates.

Those early trips probably explored Boat Cave, Skylight Cave, Rood's Glen and other inlets. Cold Water Canyon was blocked by fallen logs, Witches Gulch was also unnamed and unexplored. Stand Rock was very seldom seen except by land and Arch Cove was probably the upstream end of the trip.

By March 10th of the following year, the railroad was advertising the Dells in the *Wisconsin Mirror.*

In the *Wisconsin Mirror* of August 14, 1874, Captain Kingsbury tells of the first steamboat to pass through the Dells in 1844, *The Maid of Iowa.*

> "A great deal of argument ensued among the officers of the boat as to the best means of getting through the Dalles as it was feared the feat could not be accomplished safely. For steering, an oar after the manner of those used upon rafts was used without success. It was then decided that the passengers and crew should go ashore with ropes on each side to assist in pulling her through the Narrows. Everything being in readiness, with the help about equally divided on either bank, under command of Andrew Dunn, the engineer, was instructed to put on steam when the boat walked along up the stream, leaving those on shore looking after her in astonishment. She went on to the head of the Dalles where she lay up for those left behind. Those parties had a laborious task in making the three miles by land. They would explore every ravine to the river, only to find they must go further upstream. After some three hours they succeeded in reaching the boat."

The *Maid of Iowa* was a full-rigged side wheel Mississippi river boat 130 feet long, 20 foot beam and drawing about 16 inches of water. She never made another trip through the Dells.

In 1865, Henry H. Bennett returned home from the Civil War with a wounded right hand and no doubt felt his days as a carpenter were over. He learned the new science of photography from his uncle and brother and bought out the gallery business of Leroy Gates. Stereoscopic views were at the height of their popularity and so, leaving his wife to take care of the portrait business, Bennett spent all the time he could photographing the distinctive scenery of the Dells and Devil's Lake. As Bennett's views were circulated through his Studio and traveling agents, more visitors arrived by train to see the Dells for themselves.

"There is nothing more pleasant or health inspiring than to take a row boat on a good day and row up and down the river," said one Dells visitor in 1869. (Courtesy H.H. Bennett State Historic Site, SHSW)

Previous page: The Alexander Mitchell at Witches Gulch in the heyday of steamboating at the Dells in the 1880s. (Courtesy H.H. Bennett State Historic Site, SHSW)

Even after steamboats arrived at the Dells, small boats and guides to row them remained popular.
(Courtesy H.H. Bennett State Historic Site, SHSW)

In 1869, the Tanner House used a two-seated buggy to take hotel guests to the head of the Dells by land and a rowboat to float downstream for the return. In August of that year, the paper reported on these early tourists. "Most visitors do not stay long enough to go to all the points because carriages cannot go among the ravines and none but the healthy have the courage to penetrate the depths or climb their height.... There is nothing more pleasant or health inspiring than to take a row boat on a good day and row up and down the river..."

In July, 1870, "a party of students from Beloit College, including a gentlemen from Turkey, walked from Beloit." It was reported that they "saw the secluded falls at the head of the Dells." The story is told that H.H. Bennett, looking for more scenes to photograph, had walked up the ravine from the river and found his way blocked by the waterfalls in Witches Gulch. The following winter he skated up the river, cut steps in the ice over the falls and so was able to traverse the length of the Gulch.

In June, 1873, the *Wisconsin Mirror* announced the arrival of the long-awaited steamboat. "Hurrah for the steamer and jolly excursions through the Dells! Captain Wood of Quincy, Wisconsin arrived at Drinker's Landing just above the dam on Wednesday with a Steamboat. Its advent was entirely unexpected.... The boat is about 50 feet long and 20 feet wide and has a 6 to 8 horsepower engine. It is a side wheel craft built originally for a ferry boat." Captain Wood named his boat the *Modocawanda*.

In a few weeks, another steamer was shipped by rail from Madison. Its original name was *Lake City* but its owner, Captain Bell, reconstructed it and named it the *Dell Queen*.

From that time, there were always at least two steamboats in the Dells and occasional price wars. Rowboats were also in use for sight-seeing until the early 1900s. A rowboat and guide to row it could be hired for the round trip through the Upper Dells, or for a still pleasanter day's outing, tourists could ride up the river as far as Witches Gulch on one of the steamers, and then engage a guide and rowboat for a leisurely trip downstream.

Boats, either steamers or rowboats, seemed to have stopped anywhere their customers desired. In order to improve some of these walks, wooden planks were laid across the wet spots. In July of 1874, a trout pond and refreshment stand were opened in Cold Water Canyon. Here trout could be caught, cooked and served before or after enjoying the improved walk through the Canyon as far as Devil's Jug.

The *Modocawanda* passed into the hands of Captain Walton McNeel in 1875, who continued to operate her in the Dells until 1876. Meanwhile, the *Dell Queen* proved inadequate so, during the following winter, she was dismantled and an elegant and spacious boat was built to take her place.

This boat was also named the *Dell Queen*. Under Captain Bell, it plied the Upper Dells for the next three seasons. On June 4, 1878, she caught fire, but a large force of men rebuilt her in short order and on July 4, she made her first trip, after which she ran regular trips for the next two years.

In the meantime, Captain A. Jones brought a small steamer to join the growing Dells fleet. The 21 ton vessel, *Champion*, had been built in 1867. During the summer of 1875 she steamed up as far as Arch Cove, also called Paradise since it offered shelter from rain and a lovely bubbling spring. From Arch Cove some passengers walked to Stand Rock, quite a rugged hike through brush, swamps and across small streams. The steamer then took its passengers across the river to Witches Gulch where they walked from the cliff at the entrance to the Gulch, past Diamond Grotto and on to Fairy Grotto.

In 1878, the steamer *Alexander Mitchell* was built in Kilbourn City by the Kilbourn Boat Company, sharing business with the *Dell Queen*.

An account in the *St. Louis Post Dispatch* of June, 1879 describes an unusual boat trip:

"Dells of the Wisconsin. Nowhere in America, or in the world can more weird, wild, entrancing scenery be found condensed within so small a space. Lying as these marvelously picturesque and beautiful scenes do, within an eight hour run of Chicago....It is strange they have not long since taken rank among the world's most famed resorts for lovers of nature, but it is only four or five years since they began to come into notice. Public attention has been directed to them in great measure through the efforts of three men....H.H. Bennett is an enthusiastic artist who taught himself photography and made with his own hands many of the instruments he uses....Captain John Bell of the jaunty little steamer, Dell Queen is the second of the worthy trio....And the third is W.H. Finch of the Finch House, one of the daintiest little hotels in all the Northwest."

The neat little steamer Dell Queen II and two admirers at the Narrows in the 1880s. (Courtesy H.H. Bennett State Historic Site, SHSW)

The writer was pleased with the "Charming" village of Kilbourn City and continues, *"After a dainty breakfast at Finch's Hotel, a council of war was held. The river was booming along under a tremendous rise at the rate of twenty miles an hour. Immense rafts were rushing past every few minutes....Captain Bell decided it would be unsafe to attempt to run his tiny steamer up such a stream, but promptly proposed that he and artist Bennett should take a splendid four-oared rowboat to the head of the Dells, five miles above town while Mr. Finch should drive us up in a carriage. They then would take us in and, after pulling us to the chief points of interest give us the thrill of a lightening express run down the river with the current through the Narrows."* All the party survived this trip with even their adjectives undiminished. The writer concludes, *"Next day with Bennett, Charley Snider and Captain Jim Christy, I went over the falls [the dam] on a raft, a wild plunge amid creaking timbers."*

It was this reporter who described the river in the Narrows as a hundred feet deep and "running on edge."

The side-wheeler steamboat *Eolah* appeared on the scene in 1883.

By 1886, F.A. Field, a local grain and farm produce dealer, age 29, bought the steamboats *Eolah, Alexander Mitchell* and the *Dell Queen* and organized the first Dells Boat Company, which he sold to the Dells Resort Company in 1892.

F.A. Field built the *New Dell Queen,* the third steamer with this name, in 1888. She was 35 tons, 86 x 16 x 2 1/2', and was in service until 1898.

Captain D.C. Van Wie and his wife started buying property in Cold Water Canyon, which included the open space beyond and up to Fat Man's Misery. In July, 1895, the president of the Milwaukee Athletic Society wrote to Van Wie with final specific instructions for their excursion to the Canyon, where they were about to spend their entire day:

...you must have rapid and good waiters also... have everything look as clean and neat as a pin.... As far as meals are concerned, don't be stingy, but have plenty of everything. I think that you will have about 85 or more guests for dinner and perhaps 120-130 for supper.... I have had some pretty sad experiences in the Gulch when on my last trip to Kilbourn. If our Excursionists would have to eat such poor meals as I had there in the Gulch, they might throw me into the river and

The Alexander Mitchell and the Eolah met at the Larks Hotel in the 1880s. (Courtesy H.H. Bennett State Historic Site, SHSW)

walk back to Kilbourn. Beer-I beg your pardon-Watertown Ginger Ale-you must have plenty. I bet my straw hat against a $20.00 Gold Piece of yours that you will not have enough on hand for two hours.... I also wish you would serve coffee, good strong coffee all day... and cake should be on hand at least in the afternoon...."

The newspapers published on the day after the excursion contain no reports of anyone having been thrown in the river so Van Wie must have provided good food and all the "ginger ale" requested.

The year 1890 marked the end of one era in the Dells and Kilbourn and the beginning of another. The last lumber raft floated down the Wisconsin. H.H. Bennett placed his first order for postcards and—much to the dismay of his wife Evaline, who cried all night afterwards—ordered $100 worth of "Indian" baskets and dolls for sale to tourists as souvenirs.

Bennett also prepared a new booklet entitled, *Wanderings by a Wanderer*. Designed to be sold on the steamboats, it had a page for group pictures made that day. The publication turned out to be popular and was sold for several years. It was the first in a century's worth of Bennett Studio guidebooks which are still published today.

A New Era Opens

That a new era was opening at the Dells became evident when Colorado real estate developers John E. and T. F. Godding, entered the scene. They put up $60,000 to incorporate the Wisconsin Dells Resort Company, purchased the three steamboats of the Dells Boat Company and valuable real estate upstream.

The new company also purchased the new pier and building Captain Bell had been building at the foot of Broadway.

This frame structure had "an elegant reception room" on the street level with a ticket office. A long enclosed stairway led down to the pier eighty feet below, from which passengers boarded the steamers for the river trip. Goddings also brought a new sternwheel steamer, the *Germania,* to Kilbourn. Built in Osceola, Wisconsin in 1887, she measured 68 x 13 x 3'.

With a new boat and boat landing, the railroad improved the approach to the Dells with plantings of grass, shrubs and trees at the depot. A gravel path led down the embankment to the landing building. The music of a five piece orchestra from Milwaukee made the trips more festive and the river guides formed an association. The railroad planned several excursions to the Dells, with tickets to Kilbourn and return at the price of a one way fare plus 50¢ for a boat ticket. A dining hall on the south side of Artist's Glen was expanded and a foot bridge built across the Glen entrance.

"Wisconsin's Saratoga. Wonderful changes have produced wonderful results. The Dells Resort Co. has transformed the Dells," proclaimed the local newspaper.

Guy Glazier, an "old river rat," reminisces about one of his trips working on the New Dell Queen or "Old Betsy" as the crew called her:

"That year we got away to a good start and all was going well. Then it happened. [First Mate] Ike Bullis got an invitation to a wedding down at Rio or some place down below Portage and had to get some one to sub for him that day. So he chose Dee Olderr and Ike's last words before he left that morning were, "Now Dee, for God's sake, don't wreck Old Betsy.

"We made the morning 9 o'clock trip all safe. Coming back down river it was Captain Snyder's habit to steer the boat down thru the Narrows, then hand the wheel over to the mate while he would go below to collect the tickets. That is what he did on the afternoon trip. As he entered Circle Bend (near the Navy Yard) he passed the steering wheel over to Dee and he went below. I had just come up the front stairs with my hands full of those rustic pine cones which I sold as Dells Souvenirs, when all of a sudden I noticed the boat turning to the right and heading for the rocks. Captain Snyder passed me at a bound and with three strides went up the pilot house steps, grabbed the wheel and rang for reverse engines. Mr. Eggleston reversed the engines and got about one turn of the paddle wheels. But the boat struck the rocks near the Lower of the Twin Sisters. The impact threw the fireman ashore and that place has always since been known as "Murphy's Landing."

In the 1890s, the "elegant reception room" of the Dells Boat Company stood at the top of the stairway that carried visitors to the steamboat landing below. (Courtesy H.H. Bennett State Historic Site, SHSW)

"The steam pipe was broken a few inches above Eggleston's head, thereby saving his life. The crash of the impact, the noise of all that boiler full of steam escaping threw the passengers into a panic. Several of them started for the wheel house to go overboard, but I waved my canes and shouted, 'back, back, there is no danger now and no need to get wet'.

"When the Captain came down I went to him and said, 'Captain, shall I go for the other boat?' He said yes, so I went to the lower deck where the only skiff we had was pulled up on deck. I grabbed the bow and pushed it over the side and jumped in as it hit the water. But oh, the heart-rending wail, 'They've taken the only boat and gone with it, leaving us doomed on this ship-wrecked steamer'. By now the Dell Queen was floating majestically down stream and was perfectly safe as her hull was not much damaged."

In 1894, the first small powered tour boat made its appearance, a precursor of things to come. The Olson Boat Company started with the *Wisconsin*, owned by Ben Olson, John Soeldner and George Wenkman. This boat was like a miniature stern wheel steamer and could hold perhaps 12 passengers.

In October of 1895, seven thousand people visited the Dells on excursions and the boats had carried fifteen thousand paid passengers at 50¢ each. Some excursions were held over in town until after supper to the profit of the community.

A party from the Apollo Commandery of Chicago visited the Dells in August of 1897, stopping at the Glen Cottage where George Crandall and the Resort Company made their stay enjoyable with boat rides, a drive to Devil's Lake and a dance at the hotel. It was hoped the Dells would become a resort for Masonic societies. An Apollo club house was to be built in the Narrows and for some time the hill proposed as the site of this monstrous structure, from which there is a fine view upstream through the Narrows, was called Apollo Hill.

The Comet gasoline launch heading upstream with a youngster wearing an "authentic" Wisconsin Dells souvenir about 1910.
(Courtesy H.H. Bennett State Historic Site, SHSW)

The Resort Company had purchased much land from this hill, up the east side of the Narrows, into Artist's Glen and the north end of the Narrows where they built the Larks Hotel.

Some of it was plotted into two subdivisions-Artist Glen and Glen Eyrie. Four cottages were built in 1898. Two still stand today.

The July 2, 1898, ad in the *Mirror Gazette* heralds all these grand changes, "Apollo Commandery, K.T. of Chicago will spend a week at the Dells, commencing July 16. This famous Masonic organization will come in a body, bringing ladies and friends and camp near the Narrows. During the week they will have drills and athletic exercises with music. It will be the grandest outing ever given by this society, [and] the grandest week ever known in the Dells."

Add to all this the excitement of a new steamboat, the *Apollo,* named in the Commandery's honor. Built in Kilbourn City, she was 90 x 21 x 4'. The christening and maiden voyage of the craft was set for the week in July when the Apollo was having their festive camping party in the Dells. It turned out to be a day of turbulent weather and a storm with high winds blew the *Apollo* on shore at the start of her first trip.

The Dells Company seemed to know Buffalo Bill Cody. Probably the most well-known American in the world, he visited the Dells and was given property in the new subdivision. The developers hoped to cash in on his endorsement, but nothing much came of it.

The new century brought the automobile to Kilbourn and changed the resort business and life in America forever. As families arrived in their automobiles, smaller boats carried smaller groups. In 1901, Mr. William Blatchley added a new boat to the sight-seeing fleet, his naptha launch *Altamont.* Captain Snider, the old steamboat pilot, seeing one of these small craft moored beside the *Apollo,* exclaimed, "Polly's got a pup." In 1905, H. Goedecke and Charles Borcher reported that they had a new "vapor launch," adding to the "flood of gasoline launches which are becoming like a mosquito fleet in the Dells." Some people also knew that one could see more from a launch than from a wide steamboat, but an extra 50¢ toll was charged for using the Dells Company's landings.

That same year, Nat Wetzel came to town to manage the Dells Resort Company for the Goddings. A flamboyant character, Wetzel was sent to Kilbourn to increase the business of the Resort Company so the Goddings could profitably sell it. By way of "improvement," he white-washed the lower trunks of the pines at the Larks Hotel. He also put a raccoon in a cage. It escaped. He put a sea lion in a tank and it died. He also supposedly kept a hippopotamus in the ravine north of Birchcliff Hotel. It also died. He added a tavern and sold liquor on the boats. As a result, one excursionist is supposed to have fallen from a boat near Gates Ravine and drowned.

In July, 1908, Nat Wetzel announced that the "Dells was closed," meaning that the Dells Resort Company was shutting down since the railroad would no longer grant excursion rates. "The Dells resort will be permanently closed within the next thirty days and the property will be offered for sale. We will wind up our affairs and seek more renumerative fields."

For three years they had encouraged the dam and the manufacturing it would bring, knowing that they would sell their property to the Southern Wisconsin Power Company for flowage rights. Wetzel's announcement that the "Dells was closed," brought an angry response from J.E. Jones in the Illustrated Events. He wrote, "Things have never looked bigger and brighter for the resort than they do now,"

After the Dam

By October, 1908, the dam was completed and the water was rising. It would eventually raise the water level 17 feet at the dam site. There were many changes evident in the Upper Dells the following summer. Cliffs lost some of their striking height. Lost beneath the water were Boat Cave, Bass

Cove, Diamond Grotto and Giant's Hand. The old river bed, formerly a creek and ponds, was now navigable all around Black Hawk Island.

Witches Gulch became more accessible when the river backed up and new walks were built. "Rood's Glen is now accessible to boats and is the prettiest nook on the entire river, being just wide enough to allow the largest launches to enter....Above the Dells for ten miles the river is like a lake and boats of any draft can easily navigate without any difficulty from sand bars or other obstructions. Stand Rock is easily accessible by boat instead of the walk of almost two miles as heretofore."

However, before the dam raised the water level, the Power Company had neglected to cut the trees on the islands at the head of the Dells. That winter, with the water raised and frozen over, farmers came out to cut the trees standing above the ice, leaving a vast forest of submerged stumps a distinct threat to boat propellers. Channels were marked, but old timers are still wary of these hidden monsters.

Tourists began coming to the Dells in their motor cars in smaller groups. George Crandall had purchased a small boat, and in 1911, along with Clarence Bennett and Glenn Parsons, he formed the Dells Launch Company with the *Neptune,* the *Comet,* and the *Anona.* Two years later when Crandall bought the steamer *Apollo* and the motorboat *Seminole* and gave them to the company for $1 each, the group became the new Dells Boat Company.

Trouble started when the competitive launches began to take some of the Dells business and the operators used the walks, docks and holdings belonging to the steamboat operators.

"A river fight ensued." The solution to the problem was a landing fee which was placed on top of the 50¢ adult boat fare: naturally children rode free.

While launches were increasing, in 1911 the Rowboat Livery was still doing business. The Municipal dock area was and still is city property as it is an extension of Eddy Street. Anyone could dock a boat there for a fee. In 1912, the city was requested to build a concrete stairway from Broadway down to the dock.

World War I brought a tourist boom. Travellers came by train, bus, motorcycle and car. By this time there were many boats and boat companies and competition was fierce. Though most of the boat

The steamer Apollo at the Larks Hotel, about 1900. (Courtesy H.H. Bennett State Historic Site, SHSW)

Lunch and souvenirs were available at the Witches Gulch concession stand in the 1880s. (Courtesy H.H. Bennett State Historic Site, SHSW)

tickets were sold through the hotels and rooming houses, tourists were still harassed as they walked down the streets. In 1918, an ordinance was passed prohibiting any soliciting on the street for business with any hotel, boarding house, resort, steamboat, launch or other vessel or vehicle. Aggressive ticket sellers were already waiting on the bridge into town. They would jump on the running boards of cars approaching the bridge, urging passengers to buy boat trip tickets. Some pushed salesmanship to the limit, asking, "Do you have your tickets to get into the Dells?"

During the big storm of 1922, the steamer *Apollo* sunk at the landing. A new steamer was needed if large crowds were to be carried through the Dells. The Dells Boat Company built a new 300-passenger steel boat, 110' x 22' x 4'.

The first rivet was driven on May 13, she was launched on June 13 and christened in early July. After the christening, three hundred guests came aboard for the first trip up the river. It was short. Opposite the Swallows Nests the boat nosed up on a sandbar. Some of the passengers remembered a similar accident when the Apollo made its maiden voyage some 24 years before. No damage was suffered and trips on the following two days, with four or five hundred passengers, were made very successfully.

In 1922, the city granted permission to Grover Olson and Edward Marlow to build the municipal dock on Eddy Street "for public landing of passengers." It was completed in time to accommodate the boats of three new companies—River Boat Line, Tourist Boat Company, Consolidated Boat Company—all organized in the 1920s. Many hotels along the river also owned boats and ran a few trips a week for their guests. In 1929, the construction of Lake Delton made another boat trip possible. After taking the Lower Dells trip, the boat could travel up Dell Creek to the Lake Delton dam. Here one transferred to Lake Delton boats for "another delightful trip," including a walk through Lost Canyon. At the Mirror Lake dam another transfer was made "for a scenic trip up this charming body of water."

In 1931, the steamer *Apollo* burned and sank near the mouth of Witches Gulch.

This left the *Winnebago* as the last steamboat on the Wisconsin River.

In 1932, the country was in the depths of the depression. Visitors who could afford a vacation had to pinch their pennies, so the Silver Dollar Boat Line invented the "non-stop" trip.

The charge was $1 for the trip while the three stop trips, at Cold Water Canyon, Witches Gulch and Stand Rock, were $1.50. Tourists saved time and money.

Ed Tangney was a fulltime ticket salesman and he made money. He received a 25¢ commission on each $1 ticket. If he sold ten in a day, he made $2.50. Many men were working for $1 a day then. His expenses were minimal. He slept in a tent where the public boat launch now stands. He got his meals at Wenkman's Restaurant because he recommended Wenkman's to his passengers

Ed credits his success as a ticket salesman to copying the style of Cliff Zahler, "the greatest salesman of them all." Cliff worked for the Riverview Boat Line in a booth on the far side of the bridge. He dressed as much like a policeman as he dared, with some kind of badge on his boat cap. "He had a way of stepping out and throwing out his cane. Cars would stop. It worked. Cliff always had something complimentary to say about people's cars to break the ice."

Of his pitch to potential customers, Ed said, "Well, of course, if they didn't know about the $1.50 trip, I didn't bring it up. But if they did and if they were older people, I said, of course, there's some pretty heavy climbing to do out there. We have smaller boats and they get in closer and you can see better. We did go into Rood's Glen....and I told them we take you into one that they can't. You can see Stand Rock better than you can by walking up there. It wasn't hard to switch them. Our biggest problem was the old boat we had." Sometimes it was hard to start and many misfortunes could befall it once it did start.

46 "THE DELLS"

The Lower Dells

The Lower Dells boat trips were the special concern of Walter "Bud" Stanton. This was a shorter no-stop trip which had been popular since the beginning of tourist travel. Some of the boats in the Lower Dells were *Na-Hu-Nah, Josephine, Ramona, Red Bird* and *White Eagle*. Sunset trips were especially popular often with an Indian singer guide such as Johnny White Eagle. In 1936, a few new boats applied for licenses: the *Iris, Alvin, Wanderer,* and Finch Boat Line, for a total of 30 launches.

In the 1930s and '40s, warm summer evenings were wonderful downtown. Tourists and natives alike might start out the evening lining the sidewalk on the railroad bridge to watch the steamboat load up for its evening trip to the Stand Rock Indian Ceremonial. Ralph Connor would wave from a window high up in the Dells Boat Company building, the final warning whistle would blow, lines were thrown off and the boat was on its way. The crowd gradually moved up town where they might play bingo near the theater and perhaps win a radio or an "Indian" blanket. Movies and dancing at the Wharf were popular and an ice cream cone at Bauer's and O'Neil's was 5¢. There were band concerts one night a week and occasional water fights when the Kilbourn Fire Department challenged nearby towns. One of the favorite sports was watching the funny tourists and no doubt they equally enjoyed watching the funny natives.

During the war years from 1942 to 1945, gas was in short supply and was rationed. It was a problem to get enough to run the launches.

The crowds waited in long lines for Greyhound buses, service in restaurants outside the movie theater and on the ramp leading down to the docks for a boat trip. On weekends the crowds were usually swelled with soldiers on weekend passes from nearby camps.

The Sunday of Labor Day weekend in 1945 was the first holiday after the end of World War II. Wisconsin Dells was so crowded with tourists that guide boat captain Roger Stroede and his river guide, Bud Gussel, ran five complete Upper Dells trips, with the first starting at 7:00 AM. It was a sign of the postwar prosperity to come.

Steam was becoming a thing of the past and in the winter of 1948, the Dells Boat Company converted the *Winnebago* to diesel and it became the *Clipper Winnebago,* still in service.

When Jack Olson came home from the Navy in 1946, he urged his father, Grover, to buy steel boats to replace the wooden launches. Olson's *Chief* was the first double-decked steel boat in the Upper Dells.

Ducks, the army surplus land and water vehicles, were first brought into Lake Delton by Mel Flath in 1946. He operated a tourist trip from land near the present Mexicali Rose until 1952. In 1954, the Olsons and Hellands bought three ducks and ran them in Mirror Lake. The Hwy 12 duck dock was built in 1954. From here these World War II vehicles gave their passengers a fun ride through the woods up hill and down dale, splashed into the Lower Dells below Echo Point, into Lake Delton, past Dawn Manor and old Newport and wind through the woods and canyons.

In the 1960s, Ardell Abrahamson and Jerry Matthews, art teacher, tried to revive steamboating by building the Apollo II at Wisconsin Dells. She was an exact replica of the first Apollo. "this was accomplished by the salvaging of artifacts from the sunken boat, working from old photographs and diving to the hulk in order to obtain accurate measurements.

Design faults and clumsy handling limited its trips to the Old Dell House and back. In the following years rudder depths were changed and extra keel was added. Meanwhile the owners were insolvent and the Reedsburg Bank attempted to run her.

Finally, the Apollo II was hauled out to sit and rot on dry land near Holiday Shores Campground. It burned on June 9, 1991. As Ardell Abrahamson left town in defeat, he told his friend, "It was a noble thing to have done."

Such is the history of tour boats at Wisconsin Dells.

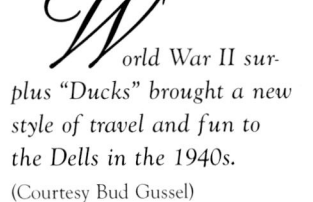

World War II surplus "Ducks" brought a new style of travel and fun to the Dells in the 1940s.
(Courtesy Bud Gussel)

"Holy Rest and Recreation—at Ordinary Prices"

"In the formation of new villages, the usual order is first a blacksmith shop, then a sawmill, and after that other enterprise demanded from the situation," noted an early Columbia county history. "In Kilbourn City, the first thing was a newspaper, second a carpenter shop, and third a hotel." The hotel arrived in the winter of 1855-56, hauled by oxen from Newport to what would be the corner of Oak and Broadway. The owner, Captain John Tanner, had decided to go into the hostelry business when visitors told Mrs. Tanner her cooking was "so excellent that she should open a hotel." Legend has it that the first paid meal in Kilbourn was served while the building was still on the mover's rollers.

Known successively as the St. Nicholas House, the Tanner House, and the Finch Hotel, this was the premier hotel in the Dells for much of its long life.

Other hotels were soon established. The Forest City Hotel flourished briefly before disappearing with the forest. The Railroad House (later known as the Commercial, the City, and Stanton's) was built by Carl Moeller in 1857, across the street from the depot. The American House went up next door in 1860; it eventually became the Hile House. These were commercial hotels; the early tourist traffic was too sparse to support a seasonal establishment.

When the Civil War broke out, the hotels became recruiting centers. In Kilbourn City, S.S. Landt recruited volunteers at the Tanner House; he later recalled that staunchly patriotic Captain Tanner provided him with "the best accommodations at a reasonable price." In Delton, Vosler's hotel was now owned by Justus Freer, who changed its name to the Union House and housed the rambunctious boys of Company E in the big ballroom upstairs. The recruits who would become some of Sherman's toughest soldiers tested his patriotism severely. They staged nightly pillow fights and midnight initiations, jumped on the beds, and generally wrecked the place.

Moved by wagon from Newport in 1856, the Tanner House was the first hotel in Wisconsin Dells.
(Courtesy H.H. Bennett State Historic Site, SHSW)

Tourist Hotels

By the 1870's, the steamboats and publicity had increased the tourist traffic significantly.

The Tanner House, newly purchased by Reedsburg innkeeper W.H. Finch and rechristened the Finch House, advertised widely that it had been "remodelled and refurnished throughout." The Kilbourn City Cornet Band was engaged to serenade guests from the balcony. Finch's improvements paid off; by 1880, he was entertaining 3500 visitors a year.

Glen Cottage was the first truly seasonal tourist hotel. It began as the seven-room home of John Vliet, president of the Wisconsin River Hydraulic Company. By 1875, J. H. Dunn was advertising its beautiful view of the river and convenient location near the steamer landing.

In 1901, after experimenting with other ventures including the Larks Hotel up the river, the Crandall family bought the property from the Dixons and renamed it the Hotel Crandall. It eventually surpassed the Finch as the top hotel in the Dells, and outlasted it, operating until the 1970s.

A handful of other hotels followed Glen Cottage. The Farmer's Home began as a year-round farmer's hotel in 1877, but it welcomed summer visitors too. The old American remained open year-round, but was transformed from a farmer's hotel into the stylish Hile House after Adam Hile bought it.

Across town from the Hile House, Schofield Cottages had been founded by another Civil War hero, Colonel Robert Schofield.

On a big tract of land at the outskirts of town, just north of Broadway, the Schofields opened their quiet vacation resort. Today, it is the only early Kilbourn hotel still in existence; after passing through many hands, it is now called Indian Trail Motel.

The Markham also stood on the far east side of town, atop the hill at the end of Washington Avenue. It had a long and misfortune-plagued history, only a small portion of which was spent as a hotel. Originally built at Point Bluff in 1856 as a Methodist seminary which went bankrupt, the building was moved to Kilbourn in 1866. Two years later it burned to the ground; it was rebuilt, but never reopened. Instead, the property was sold and remodelled into a water-cure medical institute, which opened in 1878 and was overseen by a succession of doctors, including the husband and wife team of Drs. George and Amanda McElroy. By 1890, the institute was closed and J. B. Markham was running it strictly as a summer hotel.

The old City hotel burned down in 1892. The Park Hotel was built where its barn had stood, across from the depot on LaCrosse Street. In 1902 the Park in turn was wrecked by fire, but enough remained to rebuild it. Later, it became the Hotel Helland.

Fire was clearly a constant peril in the hotel business. Before electricity, light was provided by kerosene lamps, which were a source of both work and worry. "The office had large baseburner lamps and individual rooms each had an ordinary kerosene lamp with glass chimney," wrote Lois Crandall Musson, who grew up in Glen Cottage/The Crandall. "These chimneys had to be cleaned each day, wicks had to be trimmed and bases filled with kerosene." The kitchen was another danger spot. On one occasion, a fire started under the big wood stove while lunch was being served. According to Lois Musson, "There wasn't a delay in the service. The cook kept right on working, even adding a few sticks of wood to keep the heat up, while men with axes chopped a hole in the floor beside the stove and extinguished the fire underneath." Only one guest noticed anything wrong.

These seven hotels handled the tourists and business travelers of 19th century Kilbourn. The largest could house a hundred guests, the smallest about twenty. There were also a number of boarding houses. But as late as 1905, the newspaper warned that an anticipated party of four hundred Masons from Milwaukee "would tax hotels in the Dells and overflow into Kilbourn hostelries."

You could pay from $1.50 to $2.50 per night, depending on where you stayed; there were discounted weekly rates of $7.00 to $10.00, and most tourists did stay at least two weeks, and often all summer. Boarding houses were a little cheaper. "One important consideration of a summer at the Dells is economy," according to one guidebook. "A season here costs no more than it does in ordinary homes or boarding houses."

Visitors to the Crandall Inn were met at the depot by a motorized "jitney" in the 1920s. (Courtesy H.H. Bennett State Historic Site, SHSW)

The Finch House was the top-rated Dells hotel in the 1880s. (Courtesy H.H. Bennett State Historic Site, SHSW)

The Park Hotel.
(Courtesy H.H. Bennett State Historic Site, SHSW)

The Dells was never a classic Victorian resort. It was was middle-class and unpretentious. It emphasized comfort over elegance. The Finch proudly advertised it had been called "one of the rightest, freshest, home-likest houses we ever saw." Glen Cottage was "an attractive and pleasant home." You needn't worry about being in the latest style. "The very best people appear in check or drab travelling dresses," a travel writer assured anxious visitors. "The journey up the river...is made in a steamer and can not be satisfactory if encumbered by the restraints of dress."

Men often came along with women and children. Days were spent exploring the natural beauties of the river, hiking, picnicking, fishing or even braving the rutted roads and taking a bicycle or carriage ride through the countryside.

"The summer is not for the summer hotel, it is for the closest possible association with Nature," admonished the Ladies Home Journal in the 1890s. This was where the Dells strength lay, and soon a new type of summer place, the farm resort, began appearing up and down the river, promising "pure, sweet, holy rest and recreation - at ordinary prices."

Country Resorts

All along the road that would become Highway 13 and then River Road, farmers began taking in summer boarders. As they gradually abandoned the struggle to wrest a living from the sandy soil, their farms evolved into full-fledged resorts. A few resorts grew up elsewhere - Walmar Lodge across the river (later known as Pa-lea-rida/Raftsmen's/Rustic Pines/Cambrian Lodge); Pine Glen and Ravenswood in the Lower Dells; the Blue Mound Resort; and later Multnomah on the east end of town - but "Lucky 13" was the heart of resort country. Meadowbrook, Birchcliff, Orchard Farm, Leute's Dells Farm/Artist's Glen, The Larks/Dells Inn, Berry's Cold Water Canyon, Butternut Lodge, The Pines, Rood's Glen, Chula Vista, Kriegel's, Tenney's Riverdale Farm, Atcherson's - from the edge of town up to Plainville, the highway was lined with resorts. Leute's was the oldest, and may have been taking in boarders as early as the 1870s. The former farms were set close to the road. Only places like The Pines, which had been planned as resorts from the first, were built close to the river.

Good fresh farm food was a major drawing card of the resorts, which provided three hearty meals a day on the "American Plan". The farm wives were used to cooking for crowds, and they were all known as wonderful cooks.

Guests had plenty of other activities to choose from as well. Among them were tennis, archery, horseback riding, badminton, croquet, horseshoes, shuffleboard, ping-pong, bowling, and dancing. Berry's put in one of Wisconsin's first golf courses in 1923. One could go fishing, or go swimming in the river near Birchcliff and some other resorts. Starting with Multnomah in the twenties, a few resorts put in swimming pools.

The river was the main attraction, of course. Berry's, Rood's Glen and other resorts operated their own launches and boat trips. Hiking was another big activity. "Beautiful walks to Cold Water Canyon, Artist's Glen, Rood's Glen, and Witches Gulch" advertised Butternut Lodge; as many people walked into Witches Gulch and Cold Water Canyon as landed from the river. Paths along the river were well-worn and easy to follow.

Vacationers stayed at least a week or two, some stayed all season and they usually came back to the same resort year after year.

At Birchcliff, a different group activity was scheduled each day of the week - a first night get together, the boat trip, the Indian Ceremonial, a picnic at Rocky Arbor, marshmallow roasts and square dancing. "When the Ducks first started, they would come right up here to the lodge and pick up our guests...as many as one and a half Ducks would fill up right on our property and then take them on down," remembered Bernice Loomis.

As the years went by, people changed, and the resorts changed with them or disappeared. Stays decreased from weeks to days to overnight. A week of hiking, swimming and shuffleboard was no longer lively enough. There were new attractions to take in, and a smorgasbord of restaurants to sample. The American Plan gave way to European Plan, meals not included so you could eat where you pleased. By the mid-sixties, vacationers no longer spent enough time at the resort to get acquainted with their hosts or fellow guests. "People would just check in and you'd never see them again," recalled Bernice Loomis with regret.

Motorcars, Motels and Rooming Houses

The heyday of farm resorts located miles from town had been possible because the automobile brought them within easy reach. But that same automobile gave birth to the competition that eventually outstripped them - the motel.

Early motorists were daring adventurers who had to carry everything they might need food, tents, gasoline, and of course repair tools. They had to camp out or find private lodging along the way. But they revelled in their freedom from railroad routes and timetables, and they heralded change. As automobiles became more affordable, motoring grew rapidly from a sport to an accepted middle-class mode of travel. In 1905, when Wisconsin began registering motor vehicles, there were fewer than 1500 in the state; by 1918, there were over 200,000.

Thanks to the Wisconsin River bridge, Kilbourn was once again an important crossroads on the main route between Chicago and the Twin Cities. "This season Kilbourn has been full of automobiles from all over the middle west, and from eastern and southern states," reported the *Kilbourn Weekly Events* in 1920, estimating that 3,000 cars visited the Dells that Fourth of July. "Hotels have had to equip themselves with bathrooms for the convenience of the dusty travellers," wrote a Kilbourn native.

In general, however, motor tourists didn't like the established railroad hotels. Arriving dirty and dishevelled from a day on the road, they were uncomfortable in the formal lobby of a good hotel. The meals and checkout times were geared to railroad timetables, not motorists needs. The car had to be parked in a garage blocks away.

An alternative was developed to meet the needs of early travelers, who were already accustomed to camping by the side of the road. Towns began offering free campgrounds with fireplaces, picnic tables, and rudimentary sanitary facilities, hoping to attract tourist traffic and dollars. Within a few years most municipal autocamps began charging a fee, partly to finance improvements expected by increasingly demanding tourists, and partly to weed out riff-raff with no money to spend. This provided an opening for private entrepreneurs, who soon took over the business.

Competition was unrelenting. Autocampers compared notes about facilities and rates, and standards rose rapidly as each owner tried to top the camp down the road. Privies were the norm one year, flush toilets the next. Cold showers gave way to hot. One idea that spread quickly was providing cabins, which protected both traveler and owner from the vagaries of bad weather. In places like Kilbourn, where tourists were likely to stay a week or more, cabins were especially popular. Soon amenities such as private bathrooms, mattresses and even sheets and towels were expected.

The Riverdale in the heart of resort country up River Road, 1930s.
(Courtesy H.H. Bennett State Historic Site, SHSW)

The cabin camp rearranged itself into a row or a horseshoe, and became the "motor court"; and as separate cabins were linked by carports and finally merged into one long low building, the "motel" was born.

Soon non-camping tourists discovered the advantages of the motor court over the traditional hotel - informality, economy, convenience and privacy. This last was a source of considerable ambivalence, however. While the average traveler enjoyed coming and going from his room or cabin without trooping through a central lobby under the scrutiny of a watchful hotel clerk each time he won-

Storybook Gardens, along with Fort Dells and the Wisconsin Deer Park, was one of the first theme attractions targeted at post World War II baby boomers.
(Courtesy H.H. Bennett State Historic Site, SHSW)

dered what the fellow next door was up to when no one was watching. J. Edgar Hoover didn't mince words; he called these places "camps of crime" and "dens of vice and iniquity."

This aspect of the business was less of a problem in vacation areas like the Dells. But all motels had to battle the image of the seedy "No-tell Motel" at the edge of town. Owners reassured prospective guests that they maintained high standards by advertising familiar brand names such as Simmons Beautyrest mattresses and Congoleum flooring.

Virtually all motels and courts at this time were Mom-and-Pop operations; a few companies tried to start nationwide chains, but couldn't keep up with evolving tastes. Innovation and experimentation continued. Did motel guests prefer baths or showers, a garage or an adjoining parking spot, a kitchenette or a nearby diner? Slowly, a standard plan took shape during the decades between the world wars.

The automobile reshaped the Dells in many other ways. Tourist traffic increased dramatically. "From the beginning of June to the middle of September all previous records of summer visitors have been broken," reported the Kilbourn Weekly Events in 1920.

The people of Kilbourn cheerfully set about providing lodging for all these new visitors and their dollars. In 1906, before the impact of the car, the paper noted that Kilbourn now boasted a record number of hostelries - which added up to about a dozen hotels, resorts, and places to stay "of more or less pretension" and half a dozen more private boarding houses. By the 1920 s, a tourist brochure listed 46 hotels, resorts, cottages and camps, and no less than 99 private homes which rented rooms to tourists.

The Delton-Mirror Lake-Lower Dells area was within easy reach of Kilbourn tourists. Chicago millionaire William J. Newman spotted the possibilities and laid the foundation for further growth by buying up land creating Lake Delton in the twenties. The Dell View was built as part of his vision of a first-class luxury resort. Cap Parsons moved his Indian ceremonial and trading post from the heart of the River Road resort country to the up-and-coming Lake Delton area in 1938. But by then the Depression had intervened. The Dell View and many other Dells Country resorts were hit hard.

Tourists who could no longer afford a week at a nice resort might be able to manage a weekend in a rooming house, though. This had always been an option. "For such as prefer the quiet of a home, private boarding houses offer all that can be desired," advised an 1875 guidebook. When the tourist traffic mushroomed in the twenties, so did the number of rooming houses. Most places went beyond renting the spare room; often the family gave up their own bedrooms to paying guests.

Roughly one out of three houses in town rented rooms for the summer. Many tourists, in turn, were pleased to find a place to stay for only 50¢ to $1.00 per person. Others haggled and complained even at those prices. It covered room only, not board, although some places offered breakfast for a little extra.

Rooming houses used a variety of strategies to bring in business. Some tried a hard sell approach. Freddie Sperbeck worked at Bert Tollaksen's cottages near the corner of Broadway and Vine. It was his job to deliver a sales pitch to incoming visitors who had not yet found rooms. Unfortunately, Freddie had difficulty pronouncing the letter "r." Female tourists who pulled up to the cottages were startled when a strange man approached them and asked, "Do you have your wombs yet?"

Smaller places might cut their rates as low as a dime a person, especially when business was tight. Competition became even rougher then and rival rooming house owners were not above telling prospective visitors that other places had bed bugs, "but not mine."

As the Depression came to an end, so did the rooming house era. People had been happy to find an inexpensive place to stay during the hard times but, as the number of cabins, motor courts and motels increased, the demand for private rooming houses diminished. Most had stopped taking in summer visitors by the 1940s.

World War II presented a new set of obstacles to the hospitality industry. Just when people had money again for a summer vacation, gas and tire rationing severely restricted auto traffic. Food was also rationed, and many locals were off to war or making good wages out of town.

An early version of the Tommy Bartlett water ski show, 1950s. Combining aggressive marketing with a new attraction, Bartlett changed tourism at the Dells. By locating on Highway 12, he helped shift tourist development to the Wisconsin Dells-Lake Delton strip.
(Courtesy H.H. Bennett State Historic Site, SHSW)

After The War

The end of the war meant prosperity and growth, but it didn't last long for little motels all across the country. Big motel chains like Holiday Inn and Ramada were being organized and taking their business.

Nationwide, many Mom-and-Pop motels found themselves elbowed out of business just when good times had finally arrived.

But not in the Dells. Some of the big chains did reach the Dells eventually, but they competed amid a thriving throng of independent motel, campgrounds and resorts. The enormous potential which had been held in check during the Depression and war years had finally been released. New tourist attractions, Tommy Bartlett's ski show, the Deer Park, the Ducks, Storybook Gardens sprang up along Highway 12. By 1962, the new interstate highway ran without a break from the Illinois border to the Dells; tourists spilled out four exits from Lake Delton to Rocky Arbor. The story of the hospitality industry from then until the present is essentially a story of remarkable growth and ever inflating expectations and prices. Motels, campgrounds and resorts spread out along the highways, filling in "the strip," and encircling Lake Delton. By the mid-1990s there were almost 130 places to stay listed in the area vacation guide. Amenities which had once been unheard of became more common, making the gradual transition from luxury to standard fare: swimming pool, heated pool, indoor pool, air-conditioning, queen-size beds, king-size beds, TV, cable, HBO, Jacuzzi, sauna, microwave, wet bar and more.

Lake Delton
A New Style of Tourism "Up Where The Pines Begin"

William J Newman, a millionaire contractor from Chicago, visited the Dells area in the summer of 1925, and stayed at the Sarrington House Hotel in what is now Lake Delton. Newman loved to walk through the hills, and gorges at sunrise and experience them at first light. He reveled in the natural beauty and healthful atmosphere of the place and thought that others would too. He quickly decided to buy the Sarrington House and make it part of an ultra-modern resort unlike any other in Wisconsin, if not the United States.

His plan for a comprehensive resort community looks very familiar today, but was very new in the 1920s. In addition to the Sarrington Hotel, which would be remodelled and renamed the Dell View, Newman's plan included a golf course, restaurant, dance hall/nightclub, an outdoor theater and a newly-constructed lake surrounded by upscale vacation homes. Swimming, fishing and boating on the river and Lake Delton, hiking through Lost Canyon and other scenic spots, as well as tennis and horseback riding, were part of the package, as was the Dells' first water slide. The new 2,000 acre Lake Delton complex would be marketed in Chicago and other large cities as a luxurious year-round resort community located "up where the pines begin."

Work on the lake began in 1926. Newman contacted county Judge Jim Hill, drew a pencil line on a map and told the judge, "buy up all that land within my pencil line." He then hired Chicago engineer Ralph M. Hines as construction manager.

Crews of men under Hines' supervision starting building the thirty-foot high dam and 1,000 feet of dike, using heavy earth-moving equipment shipped from Chicago. While most of the lake bed was flooded pasture, the south and west portions were wooded with pines that had to be removed. Dell Creek was also deepened and widened.

An air show, featuring a replica of the Ryan airplane flown across the Atlantic by Charles Lindbergh, was held at the Lake Delton Airport in 1930. (Courtesy, New Past Press Inc.)

With the construction of the lake under way Newman and Hines focused on the Dell View Hotel. The old Sarrington hotel was enlarged and refurnished. The entrance off Highway 12 was marked with statutes of mythological griffins and gargoyles removed from the Board of Trade Building in Chicago and massive balls of marble from the same building were placed at the hotel entrance.

On June 27, 1927, Lake Delton was formally opened. The grounds were crowded with spectators from near and far. Wisconsin Governor Fred Zimmerman was on hand to speak.

"When I heard that some man created an artificial lake in Wisconsin," he said, " where there are already eight thousand lakes, I thought it was my duty to come and take a look for myself." It was reported that he was not disappointed in what he saw. Mayors from Baraboo, Wisconsin Dells, along with W.C. Simons of Mirror Lake, and Adolph Kannenberg, a member of the State Railway Commission, also expressed admiration and praise.

Later that evening Newman hosted a banquet at which he revealed that he had spent $600,000 on his project already and would probably spend $1 million. He was particularly proud of his fish hatchery just upstream of the lake. It would raise up to 1.5 million "baby pike" for release into the lake and the river. Plans called for another hatchery and pond devoted exclusively to trout.

A working farm was also part of the project. As many as 2,000 chickens to supply fresh meat and eggs for the Dell View would be raised there, as well as ducks, pheasants, ponies and horses.

Dell View also had its own nine-hole golf course, with another nine planned for 1929. It was an interesting course in perfect condition, with greens among the "best in the world."

Camping was also available between Lake Delton and the Wisconsin River. There was no charge for the use of the grounds where dozens of tents were pitched. A baseball diamond was adjacent to the camp grounds, with a deer park adjacent to it, with a zoo next door planned for the future.

Further proof that it was up to date, the resort also had its own airstrip, the Lake Delton Air Port. The company plane was a Ryan-Brougham, the same model of aircraft that Charles Lindbergh had piloted across the Atlantic in 1927. Sightseeing flights were made daily and a complete aerial service station was maintained.

The airport opened on May 15, 1930 with a crowd of 5,000 present for the dedication and air show. Plans were to develop the airport as a terminal for tourists who would fly in to stay at Lake Delton and other resorts in the area.

By 1931, Newman had invested more than $1.5 million into the project and had 300 men working. Already in operation were the Purple Grackle dance pavilion, the Kerfoot House and Cottages on the lake. Its high diving tower, covered pavilion, boat launches, and docks made it a popular summer retreat. Newman also operated two sixty-passenger launches equipped with glass enclosures, life preservers, electric lights, automobile controls and 80 horsepower engines on Lake Delton. Plans called for another eleven launches, smaller speed boats, canoes and rowboats.

The Newman Stadium was also part of the package. Built near the west bank of the Wisconsin River it had 5,000 seats with 1,000 sheltered from sun and rain.

The most spectacular event scheduled for the stadium was a "Spanish Bull Fight," in August 1931. With the effects of the Depression starting to appear, Lake Delton needed a marketing push and the bull fight was it. Billed as a "death defying struggle between man's skill and brute strength", the bull fight would fill the stadium with prospective clients. Also to appear was Carr's Horse Circus Rodeo featuring 10 big acts, plus a polo game on horses.

The initial publicity for the bull fight neglected to mention that the practice was illegal in Wisconsin and throughout the United States. It was not an oversight, since the resulting controversy only generated more publicity. Newspapers throughout the Midwest carried the story and newsreel producers sent cameramen to film the "struggle."

Lieutenant Governor Henry Huber warned that "Wisconsin will not tolerate such brutality. Bull fights were in violation of the statues of Wisconsin and will not be sanctioned."

George Comings, of the state humane society, stated that, "no toreadors flaunting red cloaks will jump nimbly around the Newman Stadium Sunday if I have anything to do with it, and Sauk County Attorney William La Mar announced that "baiting" an animal was a crime with a fine of up to $100. If the animal died the penalty was ten to thirty days in jail.

Spokesmen for the promoters insisted that, despite threats from law enforcement officers, the fight would take place. On the day of the event, the stands at Newman's were filled with spectators who patiently sat through the horse acts and circus clowns. When the time came for the featured event to begin, the ringmaster "reluctantly" announced that, due to the laws of the state of Wisconsin, the bull fight would not be held. The spectators had to settle for merely seeing the bull paraded around the ring. They were unhappy, but had not been taken for any cash, since the promoters had not charged them for their seats. They didn't see a bull fight, but they did see a horse circus and clowns, free of charge.

The bull fight enabled Newman to make a big promotional splash, but it couldn't save Lake Delton from the Great Depression. The economic downturn hurt Newman in Chicago and killed the Lake Delton project. The resort company filed for bankruptcy and was sold for payment of its debts to the newly-organized Lake Delton Development Company. Owned by Judge Hill, Helmer Amundsen and Roy Hines, the Development Company struggled through the rest of the decade. By 1940, the company owed $10,000 in back taxes and was forced to sell the Dell View Hotel.

Activity was all but suspended during World War II, but picked up when peace returned. The value of lakefront property skyrocketed and in the 1940s and '50s the Lake Delton Development Company prospered. Lake Delton and the area around it developed into as much of a tourist haven as the city of Wisconsin Dells. In time the Highway 12 strip between the two villages became the center of area tourism.

William Newman didn't live to see it. He continued to visit the area and take an interest in his former development until he passed away in Chicago in 1943.

William Newman attempted to promote his Lake Delton resort complex by staging a bullfight in 1931, even though bullfighting was illegal in Wisconsin.
(Courtesy, New Past Press Inc.)

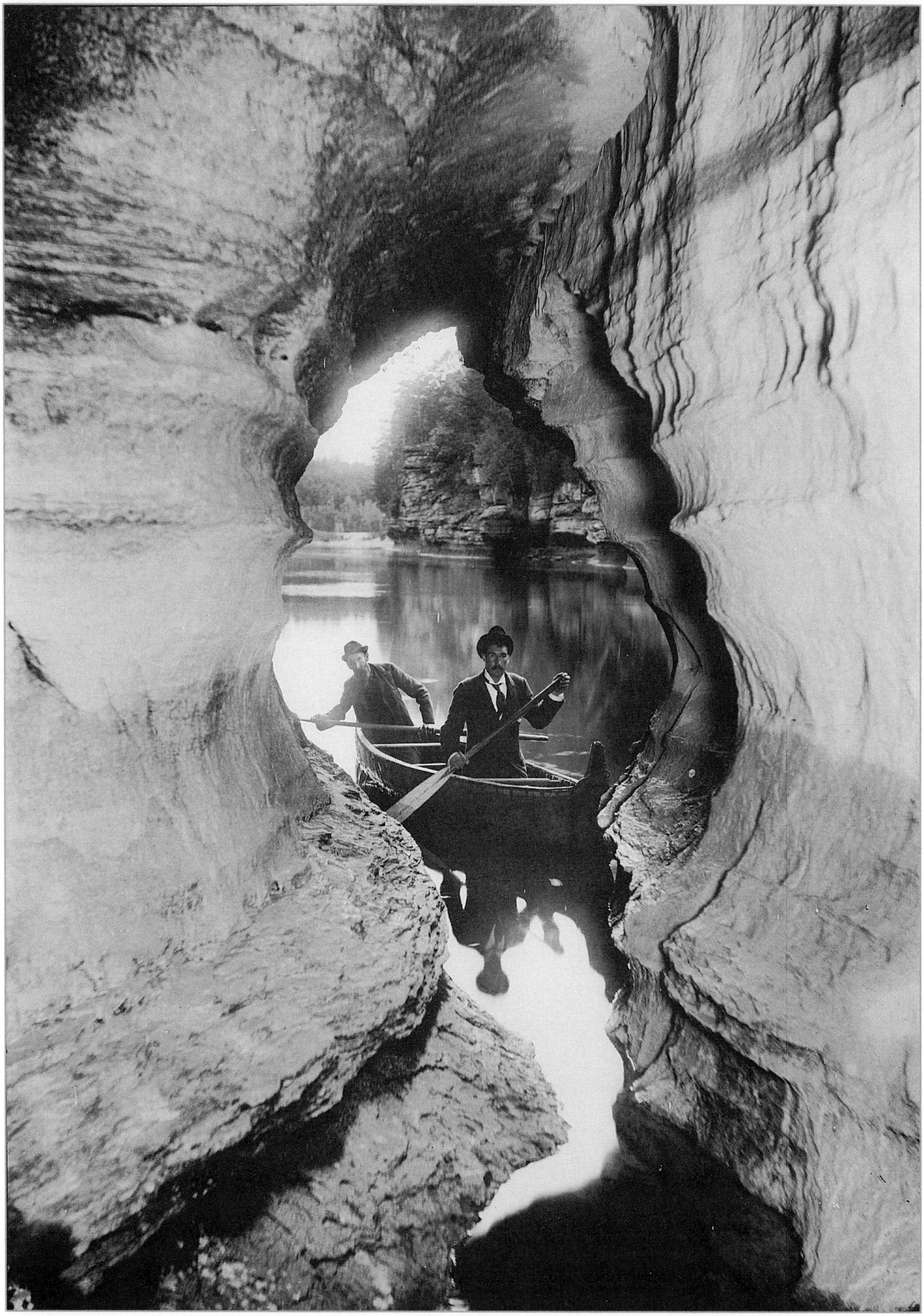

SEVEN
CONSERVATION LANDMARKS

"Uncountable Millions of Pigeons Slaughtered"

Once the most abundant bird on the North American continent, the passenger pigeon has been wiped off the face of the earth. This sad story is also an important part of Wisconsin Dells history.

The passenger pigeon was so named for its habit of passing from one part of the country to another in huge flocks. It was a beautiful bird about 17" long and pinkish gray in color. The pigeons provided meat for the table of the early colonists and the Indians, who followed their migration and camped near nesting areas. They were strong fliers, often traveling a hundred miles a day looking for food.

The stories that early settlers tell about the vast number of these pigeons seem unbelievable. In 1813 James J. Audubon watched a flock of passenger pigeons pass in a stream that lasted three days. The flock was so thick that it darkened the sun. Their wings sounded like thunder. Audubon estimated the flock to be over a billion birds.

In central Wisconsin the birds nested in jack pines and fed on acorns, wild grass seeds or newly-planted wheat. In 1871, the Dells area was the focal point of one of the largest nesting of pigeons in the eastern United States. It covered 850 square miles including virtually all of Adams County, as well as parts of Sauk, Columbia and Juneau counties. The number of birds in the nesting was estimated at 136 million. Almost every tree from Kilbourn City to Wisconsin Rapids contained 100 nests or more, so many that branches frequently broke from the weight and even whole trees toppled over.

These powerful, beautiful birds had flown from the swamps of Louisiana to central Wisconsin to hatch and raise their young. Their ancestors had made similar flights for thousands of years. It was believed that virtually all the surviving pigeons in the United States nested near the Dells in 1871. They were soon followed by hordes of hunters, trappers and egg gatherers .

In April, 1871, the Kilbourn newspaper carried this story: "The great pigeon roost this year is in Wisconsin. For three weeks, pigeons have been flying in flocks which no man could number. On Saturday, April 22, for about two hours before nightfall they flew in one continuous flock, darkening the sky and astounding people by the noise of their wings. Hotels at Kilbourn are full of trappers and hunters. Coopers are busy making barrels, and men and children are packing the birds and filling the barrels. They are shipping to Milwaukee, Chicago, St. Louis, Cincinnati, Philadelphia, New York and Boston. From 10,000 to 30,000 are forwarded daily."

Pigeons were slaughtered in every possible way. Large nets were thrown over the birds which had been baited with grain and salt. Sometimes a live pigeon was tied to a platform as a decoy (thus the term stool pigeon). While netting produced the most birds, the hunters also got their share. There are accounts of some hunters bagging over 1000 pigeons in a single day.

The adult birds provided excellent targets but it was the young pigeons—or squabs— which were most preferred. They were fatter, more tender and easier to capture. These helpless infants were pushed out of their nests with long poles or men would burn sulphur under the trees smoking them out of the nests. The trees were even burned or cut down to harvest the squabs. Squabs were so plentiful they were sold for as low as 2¢ each. School children accompanied the hunts

Millions of passenger pigeons nesting in the Dells area in 1871 brought hundreds of hunters who "slaughtered" the birds.
(Courtesy, State Historical Society of Wisconsin)

...pigeons have been flying in flocks which no man could number....darkening the sky and astounding people by the noise of their wings.

–Wisconsin Mirror

Previous Page: Boat Cave before it was flooded by the Dells hydropower dam.
(Courtesy H.H. Bennett State Historic Site, SHSW)

A monument to the passenger pigeon was erected at Wyalusing State Park in 1947. Aldo Leopold gave the following commemorative address:

On A Monument To The Pigeon

We meet here to commemorate the death of a species. This monument symbolizes our sorrow. We grieve because no living man will see again the onrushing phalanx of victorious birds, sweeping a path for spring across the March skies, chasing the defeated winter from all the woods and prairies of Wisconsin.

Men still live who, in their youth, remember pigeons; trees still live that, in their youth, were shaken by a living wind. But a few decades hence only the oldest oaks will remember, and at long last only the hills will know.

There will always be pigeons in book and in museums, but these are effigies and images, dead to all hardships and to all delights. Book-pigeons cannot dive out of a cloud to make the deer run for cover, nor clap their wings in thunderous applause of mast-laden woods. They know no urge of seasons; they feel no kiss of sun, no lash of wind and weather; they live forever by not living at all.

Our grandfathers, who saw the glory of the fluttering hosts, were less well-housed, well-fed, well-clothed than we are. The strivings by which they bettered our lot are also those which deprived us of pigeons. Perhaps we now grieve because we are not sure, in our hearts, that we have gained by the exchange.

For one species to mourn the death of another is a new thing under the sun. The Cro-Magnon who slew the last mammoth thought only of his prowess. The sailor who clubbed the last auk thought of nothing at all. But we, who have lost our pigeons, mourn the loss. Had the funeral been ours, the pigeons would hardly have mourned us.

We who erect this monument are performing a dangerous act. Because our sorrow is genuine, we are tempted to believe that we had no part in the demise of the pigeon. The truth is that our grandfathers, who did the actual killing, were our agents. They were our agents in the sense that they shared the conviction, which we have only now begun to doubt.

and were paid a penny per two dozen squabs delivered to the hunting camp.

In addition to market use, thousands of pigeons were captured alive and sold to provide live targets for shooting clubs. As the rail depot closest to the nesting Kilbourn became the center of the hunt. Trainloads of netters and shot gunners came to make their grim harvest.

As one account reads: "Embarking on the 10:00 AM train, we headed for the great pigeon roost stretching from Kilbourn City on the Wisconsin River for scores of miles beyond. Having made all needed preparations the night previous we were called to arms and headed for the roost. The idea was to get into position before daylight. The indescribable cooing produced by uncounted millions of pigeons arousing from their slumber, was heard as the hunters made up their foraging parties. Creating an almost bewildering effect on the senses, as it was echoed and re-echoed back by the mighty rocks and ledges of the Wisconsin bank. As the first streaking of daylight began to break over the eastern horizon, small scouting parties of the monstrous army of birds then darted like night spirits past our heads. Soon the skirmish line, or perhaps more correctly pigeon bummers, swept past in small and irregular bodies. Our guide now told us to get into position as quick as possible as the large flocks would follow in rapid succession. We quickly ranged ourselves along the crest of a hill overlooking a cleared valley through which the birds would fly on their outward passage.

"And now arose a roar, compared with which all previous noises ever heard are but lullabies, and which caused more than one of the expectant and excited party to drop their guns, and seek shelter behind and beneath the nearest trees. The sound was condensed terror. Imagine a thousand threshing machines running under full headway, accompanied by as many steamboats groaning off steam, with an equal quota of R.R. trains passing through covered bridges—imagine these massed into a single flock, and you possibly have a faint conception of the terrific roar following the monstrous black cloud of pigeons as they passed in rapid flight in the gray light of morning, a few feet before our faces.

"So sudden and unexpected was the shock that nearly the entire flock passed before a shot was fired. The unearthly roar continued, and as flock after flock, in almost endless line, succeeded each other, nearly on a level with the muzzle of our guns, the contents of a score of double barrels was poured into the dense mist. Hundreds, yes thousands, dropped into the open fields below. Not infrequently a hunter would discharge his piece and load and fire the third and fourth time into the same flock. The slaughter was terrible beyond any description. Our guns became so hot by rapid discharges, we were afraid to load them. Then while waiting for them others threw clubs-seldom, if ever, failing to bring down some of the passing flock.

"Ere the sun was up, the flying host had ceased. It continued scarcely an hour in all. Below the scene was truly pitiable. Not less then 2,500 birds covered the ground. Many were only wounded, a wing broken or something of the kind, which disabled, without killing them. These were quickly caught and their necks broken."

By the time the pigeon harvest of 1871 was finished, a total of 1.6 million birds had been shipped out of the Kilbourn City depot.

Another account of a passenger pigeon nesting was written by Reverend E.C. Dixon in the 1920s.

"The particular experiences which I remember most vividly began one day in the month of March, 1882. On rushing out from the schoolhouse, I saw an enormous flock high in the air and flying swiftly to the north.

"The schoolhouse faced the north so I ran around the corner to see where the birds were coming from. And there they were extending to the horizon in all directions.

"This appearance of the great flock was the beginning of a series of exciting experiences. We soon learned that the pigeons had come from Pennsylvania, for professional hunters and trappers who kept track of the movement of the flock soon appeared from the east and set in motion the whole enterprise of trapping, buying, and shipping the birds.

"It was while these flocks were out after food that the trappers got in their deadly work. The trapping was done by means of nets of about the same mesh as are used for lake fishing....The netter would place his net in an open field near to the woods. Grain was thickly strewn over the place where the net was to fall. The net itself was held back by strong spring poles of hickory or ash which, in turn, were attached to a line running back to a shelter called a bower, where the netter sat waiting his victims. Further to attract the birds a light pole was placed over the space, baited with grain and to one end of the pole a small block of wood called a stool was attached. From the trapper's bower a cord ran thru a hole in the stool to a live pigeon securely fastened at the end of the cord. When a flock was seen anywhere near, the trapper loosed the cord allowing the bird attached to it to fly into the air where its loud cries would attract the flock down to the bait. This familiar fact from the pigeon-trapping days, of course, gave rise to the phrase stool pigeon.

A Visit from John Muir

John Muir, the founder of our national park system, came to Wisconsin Dells in 1867. He had heard from botanist Increase Lapham that the rare fragrant fern could be found here. Muir and a companion located the fern in several ravines and described its aroma as most entrancing. Of the ravines Muir wrote "No human language will ever describe them." But he tried. "They are the most perfect, the most heavenly plant conservatories I ever saw." Muir and his friend stayed overnight in the Dells, then built a raft and floated down river to Portage.

"The grain and the stool pigeon lured the flock to its destruction for the birds were no sooner down upon the ground than the net was sprung and all were taken at once. The next procedure depended upon the immediate purpose of the trapper for there was an active demand for both the live birds and the dead ones. If dead ones were desired the trapper simply pinched the heads that appeared thru the meshes of the net, loaded the bodies into farm wagons and took them to town where the buyers waited for them.

"If live birds were wanted it was more difficult to take them from the nets, but many thousands were taken in that way, placed in crates, taken to town and kept in specially constructed pens until desired for shipment. There was great demand for live birds at that time for the numerous shooting clubs in the east with whom the live pigeon was a prime favorite....

"The shippers sent their produce chiefly to the great cities of the east, particularly Pittsburgh, New York, Boston, Philadelphia, and Washington.

"In June, the young birds, called squabs, were ready to gather. I say gather for it was in no sense hunting. The birds were taken much as apples are taken from the trees. And if the taking of the old birds was an atrocity, as I now think it was, the taking of the squabs was a still greater one....

With 136 million passenger pigeons alive in 1871 its hard to believe they could be exterminated in less than thirty years. Though they had few natural enemies, pigeons were vulnerable to man. They laid but a single egg a year and both parents tended the nest. If one parent was killed the egg would surely die. While the large hunts and netting during roosting killed thousands it was the unrelenting pursuit year around that destroyed the flock.

Wisconsin's last live passenger pigeon was shot near Babcock in Wood County in 1899. Two years later the last wild bird of the species was shot by an Ohio boy with a BB gun. Martha, the last living passenger pigeon died in a Cincinnati zoo in 1914.

A visitor exploring a cave at Artist's Glen before construction of the dam. (Courtesy, Bud Gussel)

"Every Rock Hidden is a Sacrilege...."

The first decade of 20th Century saw the birth of the modern conservation movement. In California, John Muir led efforts to create Yosemite and Sequoia National Parks. In Colorado, Enos Mills persuaded the federal government to create Rocky Mountain, Mesa Verde and other national parks. In Wisconsin, voices calling for the preservation of the state's natural treasures spoke in favor of creating an extensive state park system. One of these voices was that of H.H. Bennett, who vigorously opposed the building of the Wisconsin Dells hydropower dam because it would raise water levels and flood the natural wonders upstream.

In 1903, Wisconsin's first state park commission drew up plans for the first state park system. Of the three parks proposed, one contained both the Dells and Devil's Lake in a single large park. The other two parks—Peninsula and Wyalusing—were created as proposed, but the Dells portion was dropped from the Devil's Lake Park.

"My energies for near a lifetime," Bennett wrote in 1906," have been used almost entirely to win such prominence as I could in outdoor photography and in this effort I could not help falling in love with the Dells. There are few people who see them who don't become infatuated... Except with me, every rock that is to be hidden from sight is a sacrilege of what the good God has done in carving them into beautiful shapes, but very few of my good Kilbourn neighbors feel this way and most of them believe now that the Dells will be quite as beautiful with fifteen feet of them under water."

As Bennett admitted, few of his neighbors and only a handful outside of the Dells agreed with him. The promise of jobs that would be created by the hydropower dam, the promise of industry, growth and Progress that dams at the Dells had always extended but had yet to deliver was too strong to resist. Even though the Progressive era had begun in Wisconsin, the environmental era had not and the legislature acceded to the hydropower interests, and the dam was built.

"No Man Can Own the Dells."

In March of 1892, a young man stepped off the train to begin his new job as night operator at the Kilbourn Depot, wages $45.00 a month. Within a year he married Nellie Bennett and was soon looking for ways to add to the family income. He advertised as an agent selling sewer and drain pipe, tried furniture sales and undertaking. In 1895, the Crandalls made their first venture into the summer resort business. They rented Glen Cottage, a seven room house on the southwest corner of River Road and Wisconsin Avenue, and converted it into a small hotel. In 1898, George tried the furniture and undertaking business.

In 1898, the new Dells Resort Company asked the Crandall to manage their Larks Hotel, later the Dells Inn, at the head of the Narrows between Artist's Glen and Cold Water Canyon. George also managed hotels and properties in Texas.

In 1908, the Dells Resort Company sold its Dells holdings to the Southern Wisconsin Power Company. The power company persuaded Crandall to manage these properties, along with other river-front land threatened by logging. He supervised additional land purchases for the Company and on his own to prevent the construction of roads, hotels, summer homes and advertising signs along the shoreline. To restore the riverbank, he reforested logged over ground.

By 1944 Crandall had purchased purchased Stand Rock and the Hotel Crandall and was also a partner in the Dells Boat Company, owner of the steamer Apollo and several small launches. He shared the belief of his father-in-law, H. H. Bennett, that the natural beauty of the Dells was

"This beauty is yours because others before you loved the Dells."

its greatest attraction and should be preserved from excessive commercial exploitation. In the 1930s he encouraged the federal government to create a national park at the Dells, but died without seeing his dream realized. His life exemplified his words, "No man can own the Dells. He can only be its custodian for a time."

His wife Nellie and daughters, Lois Crandall Musson and Phyllis Crandall Connor, followed him in management of the riverfront properties, the Dells Boat Company, Hotel Crandall and the Stand Rock Indian Ceremonial.

Since neither the Mussons nor the Connors had children, they grew concerned over the future of their properties. In the late 1940s, they revived their father's idea to create a national park at the Dells, but found little support locally, in Madison or Washington D.C. State officials

The George Crandall family relaxing at the Narrows, part of the Dells scenery they worked hard to preserve.
(Courtesy H.H. Bennett State Historic Site, SHSW)

CONSERVATION LANDMARKS   61

did, however, introduce them to the Wisconsin Alumni Research Foundation. On January 16, 1954, after much thought, the Connors and the Mussons gave most of their Dells properties to WARF. These holdings included 1200 acres of land along the river, mostly in the Upper Dells, the Dells Boat Company with three launches, the Clipper Winnebago and supporting equipment, the Crandall Motor Inn, the Stand Rock amphitheater and interests in the Lower Dells. Provisions were made that these operations would continue to pay federal, state and local taxes in the four counties and five municipalities. The only building allowed on the river bank would support tour boats and their passengers. All of the donors received a small income during their lifetimes, but their greatest reward was in the knowledge that their legacy was secure.

WARF continued to purchase land in both the Upper and Lower Dells and became the single largest owner of river frontage. In 1997, the state of Wisconsin purchased nearly all of the WARF land and created the Wisconsin Dells Natural Area.

A bronze plaque erected in Witches Gulch sums up the profound contribution of the Bennett-Crandall-Connor-Musson family to the Dells: "This beauty is yours because others before you loved the Dells."

Aldo Leopold's "shack."
(Courtesy New Past Press Inc.)

"I Bought Myself a Sand Farm"

This gift came in the form of an eighty-acre plot in the Town of Fairfield which gave a University of Wisconsin professor an opportunity to answer a simple question. When the drought of the mid-1930s reduced the already-poor sand soil farmers of central Wisconsin to straits even more dire than they had always known, and the federal government was offering aid and incentives to resettle them, Aldo Leopold asked why "these benighted folk did not want to go...and finally, to settle the question, I bought myself a sand farm." The sand farm Leopold bought became the focus of his thoughts about land use and conservation. His ruminations while at "the shack" evolved into what he called his "land ethic," the ideal that asks humans to look at natural resources not merely in terms of the dollars and cents to be derived from them, but in terms of their "trans-economic value and importance." In these terms, a sandstone blufftop for example, was valuable whether or not it was a tourist attraction or suitable for sub-dividing and a plot of blowsand in Adams County was vital not as farmland but as habitat for wildlife.

In the fall of 1934, the Wisconsin Conservation Department opened a bow-hunting season for deer in Sauk and Columbia counties. Deer were much less abundant in central Wisconsin in the 1930s than they are today and the new season generated much excitement. University of Wisconsin professor Aldo Leopold, his wife Estella, and their sons Starker and Luna, tried their luck in the woods north of Lodi in Columbia county and along the Baraboo River in Sauk County near Lake Delton. The hunters were not very successful at bagging a deer. They were happy just to have seen about a dozen bucks and Leopold consoled himself with a journal entry that read, "...deer hunting is a continuous series of mishaps. If you persist long enough, there comes a time when the hap takes place without the miss."

The "hap" that took place on this hunting trip was the Leopolds' discovery that they wanted a family retreat in the country. A few months later, in January 1935, Prairie de Sac taxidermist Ed Ochsner brought Leopold to a weathered shack on forty acres of blowsand along the Wisconsin River in the Sauk county Town of Fairfield. The Leopolds purchased the shack, which had recently been home to a flock of chickens, and land around it for back taxes.

In the spring of 1936, the Leopolds began to make regular visits to the place. "...farm neighborhoods are good in proportion to the poverty of their floras," he wrote in *A Sand County Almanac,* then penned a tongue-in-cheek description of it. "My own farm was selected for its lack of goodness and its lack of highway; indeed my whole neighborhood lies in a backwash of the River Progress...My neighbors bring a sigh to the County Agent. Their fencerows go unshaven for years on end. Their marshes are neither diked nor drained. As between going fishing and going forward, they are prone to prefer fishing..." as was Leopold when he was at the shack. More likely, he would walk the blowsand dunes, the sedge marsh, or the river islands, tramp over the worn out pasture where he and his family would plant a thousand young pines and search for the simple truths nature placed there, but that only a few people, like Aldo Leopold, could find.

> "My own farm was selected for its lack of goodness and its lack of highway; indeed my whole neighborhood lies in a backwash of the River Progress..."
>
> ALDO LEOPOLD

Here was the good oak, whose felling Leopold used to reveal the history of natural resource use and abuse; here the white pine whose tender candles stretched a tentative reach to the sky; the snow-covered flats where the professor tracked a skunk whose path led "straight across-country, as if its maker had hitched his wagon to a star..." and where for a mere thirteen years of weekends, hunting trips and vacations, Aldo Leopold played, worked, reflected and wrote.

One of the pieces of writing he worked on throughout the late 1940s was a collection of essays entitled Great Possessions. In the early spring of 1948, after several frustrating years, he received word that the Oxford University Press would publish it and he planned to spend the summer revising and editing. In April, Leopold, his wife Estella and their daughter Estella, Jr., came to the shack for a weekend. The woods and marshes had yet to green up and, when a fire broke out on a neighbor's property, it threatened the young pines the Leopolds had so carefully planted and tended. All three of them rushed off to help their neighbors fight the fire. Leopold and the women split up and many hours passed before Estella, Jr., noticed that her father was missing. He had been using a backpack pump to wet the grass in front of the fire when he was struck by a heart attack. He took off the pump, laid down in the grass with his hands folded across his chest, and never again rose in this life.

His family and friends made sure that the book he was working on was published. The title evolved from Great Possessions to A Sauk County Almanac, and a A Sand Country Almanac, to the final A Sand County Almanac of world-wide fame. The Leopold family continued to use the shack as a summer home. It has been preserved as part of the Aldo Leopold Reserve and is used for conservation research. Leopold's daughter Nina and her husband, geographer Charles Bradley, have made their home on the property.

The truth is in all things," wrote the poet Walt Whitman. A generation later, Aldo Leopold found the truth of environmental awareness—both simple and complex—in the things he discovered on a blowsand farm in Sauk County near Wisconsin Dells. (Reprinted with permission, Sauk County Historical Society)

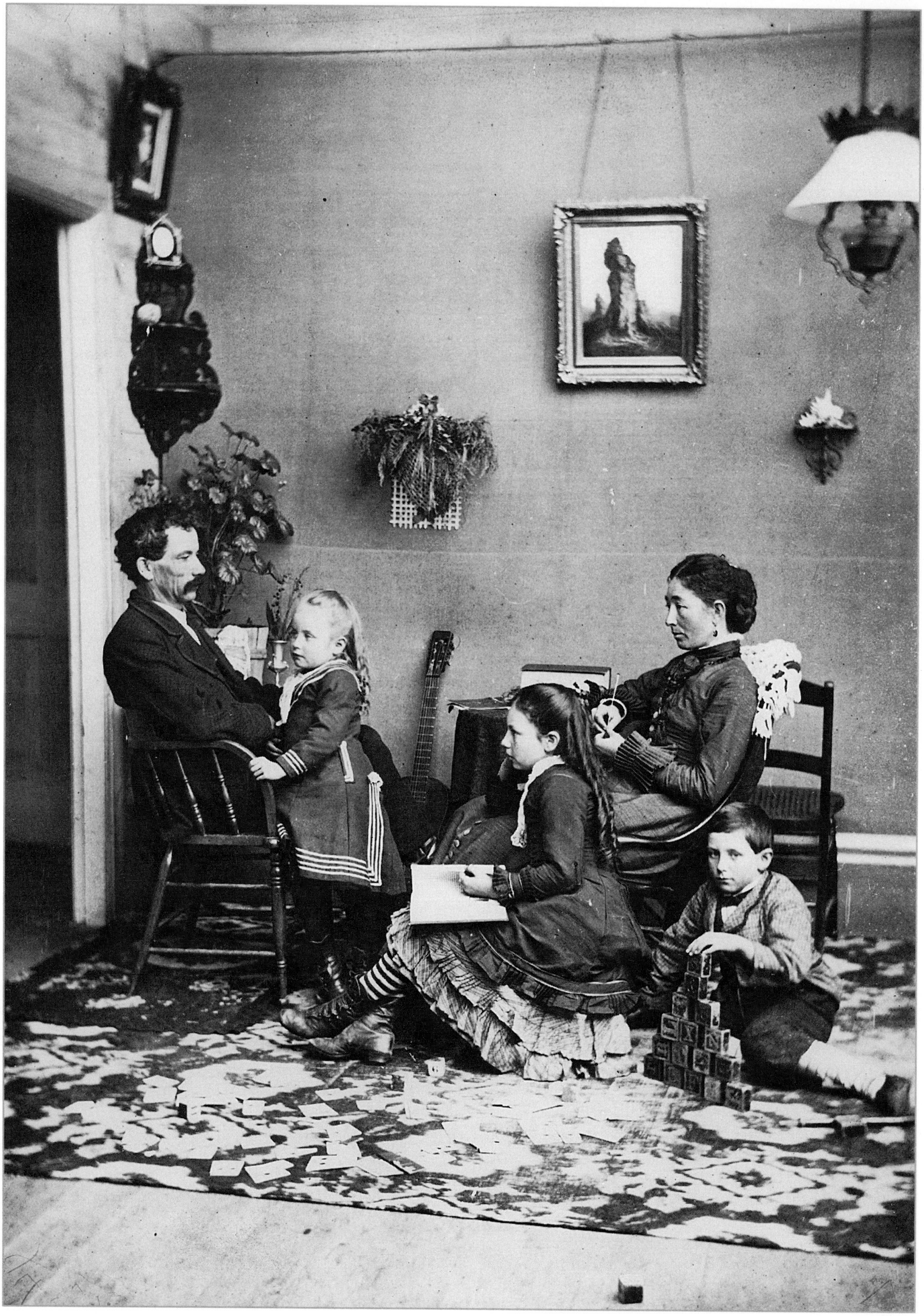

EIGHT
DELLS STORIES

The First Bridge Across the Wisconsin

By the mid-1840s, the Dell House on Black Hawk Island on the west side of the Wisconsin, was a going concern, with 100 or more rivermen spending the night and putting coins in Robert Allen's cashbox. Allen was also running a ferry that enabled settlers traveling up the Pinery Road from Portage to cross the Wisconsin and proceed up the Lemonweir Valley. After Indian land on the east side of the river opened for settlement in the late 1840s, Allen's ferry carried newcomers from west to east.

With all the traffic crossing the river, and with a lot more likely to come, Allen and a partner named Hugh MacFarlane obtained a charter from the legislature to construct a bridge across the Narrows a short distance up from the Dell House. The partners would finance construction themselves and collect tolls set at 10¢ for vehicles drawn by one draft animal, 20¢ for vehicles requiring two animals, with another nickel charged for each additional animal. Herds of cattle or horses cost 2¢ per head, but sheep and hogs could pass for a penny. Pedestrians could cross free of charge.

Allen and MacFarlane obtained the charter, but Schuyler Gates designed and constructed the bridge. He had arrived at the Dells in 1849 and quickly acquired the land on the east bank where the bridge would touch. As a young man, Gates had worked on the Erie Canal, and had helped build and manage a canal railroad in Pennsylvania. He seems to have had the basic knowledge of construction and financing to handle the bridge project.

Although the records are not exact, Schuyler Gates, with help from his son Leroy, certainly completed the bridge in 1850. They used white pine beams, some hand-hewn, some milled to build a simple but strong trussed bridge that spanned the 53-feet gap at the Narrows.

As the only bridge on the river, what became known as the "Gates Bridge" was a busy thoroughfare. "Being on the direct line of travel between eastern Wisconsin and the Lemonweir, La Crosse and Minnesota, there is an immense amount of emigration now passing over it," reported Alanson Holly's Wisconsin Mirror in 1856.

The bridge was also a popular spot from which to watch lumber rafts make their wild ride down river. Perhaps it was the presence of this captive audience on the bridge that prompted Leroy Gates to carve into the rock nearby his self-promoting declaration that he was "Leroy Gates Dells & River Pilot from 1849 to 58." (Later immortalized in a Bennett photo and still faintly visible, Gates carving may be the first in an long, long line of outdoor ads at the Dells.)

The Dell bridge carried settlers, river drivers, stage coaches, livestock, land speculators and merely curious visitors across the river until 1866. The spring break up came suddenly that year and the river rose to reportedly record levels that smashed dams, bridges and logging works up and down stream.

"Water the highest it's been for a great many years. It's terrible, awful, sublime, majestic and grand," wrote H. H. Bennett on April 23, 1866. Two days later, the flooding river had washed out the Dell bridge.

By then, most of the cross-river traffic had moved to the more conveniently-located and sometimes toll-free bridge the railroad had constructed at Kilbourn in 1857. There was some talk of rebuilding a bridge at the Narrows for the tourist trade in the 1880s, but no action was taken. Instead, the Dells bridge of Schuyler Gates will be simply remembered as the first bridge to cross the Wisconsin.

The first bridge across the Wisconsin, built in 1850.

Previous page: World-renowned Dells photographer Henry H. Bennett and his first family: daughters Nellie and Harriett, who often served as models in his photos, wife Frances, son Ashley. (Courtesy H.H. Bennett State Historic Site, SHSW)

Hops pickers at work stripping the flowers from the vines in the boom years of the late 1860s.
(Courtesy H.H. Bennett State Historic Site, SHSW)

The Hops Boom

Between 1850 and 1860, the number of breweries in the United States tripled, with Wisconsin itself having 127 beermakers. This increase created greater demand for hops, the ingredient that gives beer and malt liquors their characteristic aroma and bitter flavor. Wisconsin farmers turned to hops growing and the Dells area was the center of the industry.

Jesse Cottington, an experienced hops grower from New York, began growing hops in the Sauk County Town of Winfield in 1852. Hops are a perennial vine with roots planted at eight-foot intervals next to a 12 - 20 foot pole for the vines to climb.

Cottington imported roots from New York and supplied them to several neighbors. The combination of hops growing experience, suitable climate and soil, and an expanding market made Sauk, Juneau, Columbia and Adams counties an important hops growing area. By the mid-1860s, market conditions would create a "hops craze".

Hops required intensive culture. Each year poles were set. In late May, women worked in the hops fields, tying young vines to the poles. At the end of the summer an army of pickers descended upon the hops yards.

The brewing process uses the fluffy, yellow-green hops flower. At harvest time, men pulled the vine-laden poles and carried them to picking stations. Each picking station consisted of four large wooden boxes. A young woman at each box laboriously picked flowers from the vines. The average picker could fill three boxes a day at 50¢ per box. At $1.50 per day, a hops picker earned a little more than an unskilled sawmill worker.

In 1867, Sauk County produced at least 2,000,000 pounds of hops and some estimates put the figure as high as 4,000,000 pounds. Hops producers recruited thousands of young women from towns along the rail lines to harvest the crop. From places like Beaver Dam, Watertown, Oconomowoc, and, of course, Milwaukee, 30,000 pickers came to the four-county hops region. In describing the arrival of a trainload of pickers the Wisconsin Mirror said that "when 2,000 pickers began to pour out of every door of those twenty cars, the scene beat all other western shows."

For a three-week period in late August and early September, the people working on the harvest overran the yellow-green hops yards. Years after hops growing faded from the scene, people remembered hops picking time. Women recalled picking hops until their fingers bled, yet spending evenings singing and stepping to the lively music of nightly barn dances. Pickers enjoyed meeting new people and learning to dance the newly invented "hops step." The dancing, singing, and mingling of men and women in the carnival-like atmosphere made the long hours of harvest bearable.

Because it was the rail shipping point, Kilbourn City was the hub of the hops region. In 1859, a farmer received 14¢ per pound for hops delivered to Kilbourn. Eight years later, increased demand coupled with the damage inflicted by hops lice on crops in the East pushed the price of hops up to 65¢ per pound. Hops fever struck many farmers in Sauk, Juneau, Columbia, and Adams counties. The rush was on to plant hops roots, build hops houses, buy hops presses, and become a hops grower.

A fine line exists between investment and speculation. The price of hops in 1867 encouraged some farmers not only to invest in hops growing equipment but also to neglect other crops. Some, in the haste to plant fields of hops, mortgaged their farms to buy more land. In 1868, increased acreage and the return to productivity of eastern hops fields resulted in a glut. The price of hops crashed to 10¢ per pound and below. Growers sold their crops at a loss. Fortunes were unmade and some farms were lost. Hops acreage dropped rapidly and would fade away by the turn of the century. The "hops fever" had broken.

Bloody September, 1869

(The New York Times, September 19, 1869) *"In Wisconsin, within a mile of Kilbourn, Gates was murdered on September 13 by a man who robbed him a year before to stop his testimony. Three days later, at Portage, 17 miles east, a lawyer shot and killed a yeoman and a mob hung him instantly. Two nights later people from far and near mobbed the Portage jail and hung the robber, Wildrick, who had robbed Gates, who was murdered five days previously. Four days later Miller Davis was robbed, murdered, and thrown senseless on the railroad tracks at a railroad Station 15 miles west of the scene of the first murder where he was mangled by the train. Three days later an Indian killed a Frenchman on a cranberry marsh. The Indian is in jail and the rest of the murderers are at large. A pleasant place those regions of Wisconsin."*

As the editor of the Times sarcastically pointed out, "those regions of Wisconsin" near Wisconsin Dells could be far from pleasant. In a period of two weeks, six murders took place within a 20 mile radius of Wisconsin Dells. Four were directly related to the village and one of its most prominent citizens, Schuyler Gates. The final two, of Davis and "the Frenchman" were coincidental, but nonetheless added to the lawless atmosphere of the times.

The tale began in 1866 when Schuyler Gates, the man who had built the first bridge across the Wisconsin at the Narrows in 1850, began to sell his property and prepare for his retirement. Gates was in his sixties, so a few eyebrows were raised a year later when he married twenty-three year old Mary Ann Cusick. In May, 1868 Gates and his wife embarked on a trip to visit Schuyler's daughter in Kansas. They loaded their belongings onto several small boats and with $2,200 in cash and "marked" bonds tucked into a money belt embarked down the Wisconsin.

They were camping on an island in the river near Arena when they were set upon by two masked bandits. They pistol-whipped Schuyler and left him bleeding and unconscious, then raped Mary Ann, tied her to a tree and made off with the $2,200.

Mary Ann struggled free, got Schuyler into a boat and brought him to a nearby farm where his wounds were tended. Although he lingered "on the very threshold of death," Gates recovered and was able to testify before the grand jury that he and Mary Ann had been attacked by the notorious Pat Wildrick and his partner in crime, Pat Welch.

Wildrick led of a band of cutthroats well-known in the Wisconsin River Valley and had served time in prison for assault and robbery. He was soon arrested by Columbia County Sheriff Phidelus Pool and found to be carrying $1,100 in marked bonds and cash.

In September, while Wildrick was awaiting trail, Schuyler Gates was murdered. He had walked across the railroad bridge at Kilbourn, followed by two members of Wildrick's gang. A few hours later, a farmer traveling on the road from Reedsburg found his body.

In the communities of Kilbourn, Baraboo, Mauston, Briggsville and Portage, it was commonly believed that Wildrick had Gates killed in order to prevent his testifying at the trial. It was also commonly believed that Wildrick could not be convicted without Gates' testimony.

Feelings were already running high when Wildrick's attorney, a short-tempered, abusive man named William Spain, got into an altercation in Portage with a fellow named Barney Britt. Spain pulled out a pistol, shot and killed Britt. Hounded by a mob crying "Hang him," Spain sought protection by surrendering to the Portage city marshall, who placed him in the lock-up. The mob soon broke down the doors, dragged Spain out to the nearest tree and hanged him.

The following evening, in Lyndon Station, Mauston, Baraboo, Portage and Kilbourn, men were seen to be quietly gathering. Although the weather was warm, they all seemed to be carrying overcoats and wearing hats low over their eyes. A crowd estimated at 125-150 men gathered outside the jail in Portage. They forced open the door, tied up the sheriff and his deputy, then found the three keys necessary to open the locks on the way to Wildrick's cell. With none of the rushing and shouting that had accompanied the lynching of William Spain, the men grabbed Wildrick, placed a noose around his neck, dragged him out of the jail to a tree in a nearby ravine and hanged him.

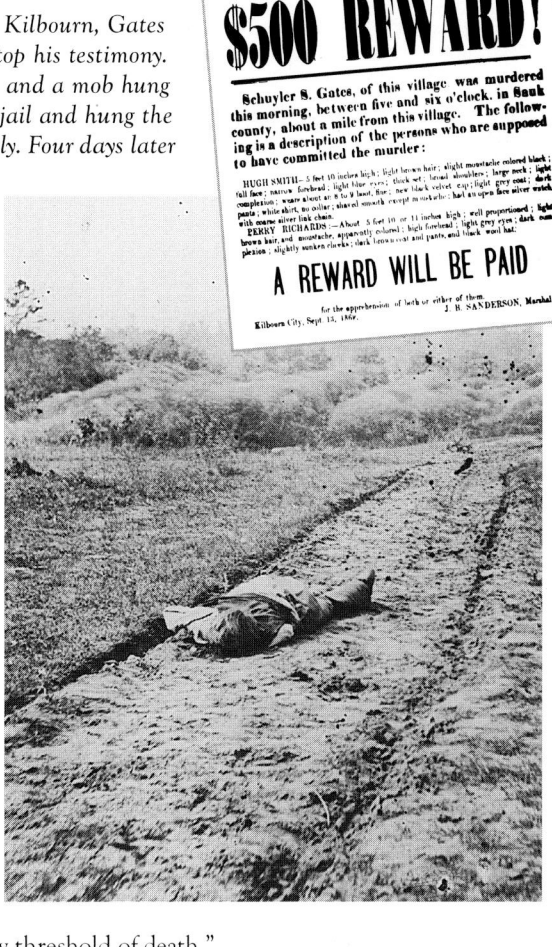

A poster offering a reward for the murderer of Schuyler Gates and Gates' body lying dead in the road near the Wisconsin Dells Railroad bridge.
(Courtesy H.H. Bennett State Historic Site, SHSW)

"His Words Bite Like Coals of Fire"

The Progressive Movement has been called the most important political movement in this century. Much of modern American government—primary elections, voting rights for women, the protection of citizens from corporate abuse, environmental awareness, public health and safety standards, child welfare and compulsory education laws, compensation for injured workers and their dependents, social security for the elderly, and the "progressive" income tax—all began as Progressive ideals.

The political figure most closely associated with the Progressive Movement is Wisconsin Governor and Senator Robert M. LaFollette. Born in Dane County, LaFollette married Belle Case of Baraboo. After serving in Congress for several terms in the 1880s, La Follette decided that the conservatives governing Wisconsin and the United States were not meeting the needs of those who elected them and should be replaced. In the 1890s his philosophy evolved and by 1897 he began to test it in public.

La Follette made one of the first statements of his philosophy at a picnic for local Republican Party members at Fern Dell, near Lake Delton. He denounced corporate control of the political system and the Republican Party for their dedication to "base and selfish aims." La Follette's fevered eloquence led one reporter to later remark that "his words bite like coals of fire."

His Fern Dell speech is hailed as one of the first steps La Follette took on the road that take him to the Governor's mansion, the United States Senate, and to the leadership of the most successful political reform movement in American history.

Senator Robert M. La Follette, who used his excellent oratorical skills to further the Progressive cause at the Dells and throughout the United States.
(Courtesy H.H. Bennett State Historic Site, SHSW)

"A Cheerful Unselfish Life"

"Dedicated to Minnie Drinker Snider and Fred B. Snider. Like a cup of cold water to fevered lips is a cheerful, unselfish life in this busy world. To two such lives, which found happiness in kindness to every living creature, this memorial is a tribute."

Early one evening in June of 1898 the members of the village board and many other interested citizens of Wisconsin Dells gathered at the site of the memorial fountain on Broadway for the unveiling of this gift from Mr. Charles Snider to the memory of his wife and brother. The local paper reported, "Little Natalie Snider, a sweet little girl of five summers, a niece of the donor, pulled the cord which released the veiling, and, as the figure and outline was revealed a cheer went up."

Charles Snider's son Harry then addressed the village board and presented the fountain in the name of his father and himself. For many years the lady of the fountain offered her gift of cool, refreshing waters impartially to birds, horses, dogs and people from her original location at the intersection of Broadway and Superior Streets. At that time Broadway did not continue west from Superior Street, but when the land was filled in so that Broadway ran straight west to the bridge, traffic became heavy and the fountain had to be moved. After trying several different locations the memorial finally found a home on the grounds of the village library.

An Auto Trip to Kilbourn

The following first person account gives a graphic story of the slow growth of auto travel as a popular means of coming to the Dells. On August 3, 1906, five Winton cars containing "happy autoists," including women and three children, started from Minneapolis to "the Delles of the Wisconsin, the party being in charge of that indefatigable worker and all around hustler, Mr. A.C. (Ashley) Bennett, ably assisted by "Dr." Dave Thomas in charge of the repair car."

The party left at 8:15 a.m. and arrived at Winona at 11:30 p.m. There were many hills, and a broken spring in one car had to be repaired by a local blacksmith. Townspeople and farmers turned out all along the way, even at 11 p.m., to see the five cars.

On the second day in the rain, some of the cars lost their way beyond Sparta and "plunged back into the wilderness and found innumerable trails thru sand and scrub oak, but little or no road...." The distance from Sparta to Tomah was only 22 miles, but it took four hours....the day's run of 92 miles was the hardest day's work of the entire trip."

It was still raining on the third day. "We had been warned of a very steep and slippery clay hill about five miles outside of town, but the first two cars negotiated it successfully. The Larabee car, however, came to grief by breaking her driving chain about half way up the hill, much to the delight of the various countrymen who passed up or down the hill on foot or in buggies. We finally reached the valley without any mishap and then had sand and mud, sand and mud through Clifton, Hustler, New Lisbon to Mauston, where we arrived at five o clock, 31 miles out....we landed in Kilbourn at 7:20 p.m. tired, wet, hot and hungry."

The fourth day was spent enjoying Upper and Lower Dells boat trips in Mr. Olson's launch and buying souvenirs. On the return trip, the fifth day, there was another breakdown but they enjoyed dinner at the Sherman House in Tomah.

Minneapolis-Kilbourn Trip Log	
Total Mileage	601 miles
Actual running time	51 hours
Average MPH	11.8
Rain	4 Days
Good Roads	210 miles
Heavy Sand	90 miles
Trails	40 miles
Mud-Chuck Holes	240 miles
Clay Hills	20 miles

The Snider Fountain when it stood at the end of Broadway in what is now downtown Wisconsin Dells. It offered a refreshing drink to all creatures great and small. (Courtesy H.H. Bennett State Historic Site, SHSW)

DELLS STORIES 69

An early automobile expedition to the Dells. The car is parked on the west approach to the combination railroad/highway bridge built in 1896. Now closed to autos, the bridge is still used by the railroad.
(Courtesy H.H. Bennett State Historic Site, SHSW)

After spending a day in La Crosse, the travelers ventured forth for the seventh day of their journey. There were a few more breakdowns and more rain. Two of the cars had to be shipped by freight to Minneapolis and their occupants also took the train home. Others had left the caravan earlier and the last two cars were separated for the final leg of the journey.

Ceremonial at Stand Rock

The start of the 20th Century saw a rise of interest in Indian people and culture, and as early as 1919, Indian dances were held at Stand Rock for the tourists. The August 5, 1920, Kilbourn Weekly Events simply states, "Several from here have been to see the Indian dances at Stand Rock."

The dances were generally held in July and ran for 10 nights. The Dells Boat Company sent steamers to the ceremonial nightly: the 1922 fare, including admission to the dance and all expenses, was $1.25. By 1924, the Indian dances had become a major attraction, and that year the event was expected to attract thousands over its 10 day run.

Captain Glenn Parsons, with George Crandall and the local Ho-Chunk group, helped organize the first ceremonial dances for tourists at Stand Rock. Parsons was general manager of the Dells Boat Company. Area Ho-Chunk appreciated his efforts to re-establish the ancient custom. Their ancestors had danced at Stand Rock for centuries, but before this revival, it had been ninety years since the tribe had practiced the annual ceremonial there. They were also honored when the boat company named one if its steamers Winnebago. Thus, in 1924, the Ho-Chunk gave Parsons the name Zazamanega, meaning Thunder Bird, and adopted him into the tribe as a chief in a very traditional and dignified ceremony conducted by Chief Little Bird. According to some Ho-Chunk, Parsons was only the second white man in Wisconsin to receive this highest honor.

In 1929, the Parsons/Crandall partnership was dissolved and Parsons developed a new Indian pageant site near his Indian Trading Post at Indian Hill on Hwy 13, now River Road. Crandall remained and the Stand Rock Indian Ceremonial was officially named and designed by his daughter, Phyllis Crandall Connor, who directed the show for the next 25 years.

That year the dances were held from June 27 to September 3, and included Indian entertainers from across the nation. According to the July 11, 1929, Kilbourn Weekly Events, some of these were "Chief Silver Tongue, a tenor of supreme quality...Evergreen Tree, an impersonator of birds and animals that has no equal...Little Moose, a dramatic reader of a type hardly ever seen, and not to be slighted is Blue Bear, a baritone singer with a voice as clear as crystal." Chief Lone Tree presided over the ceremonial and Chief Daybreak, better known as Jim Smoke, took the role of announcer. Several of these performers appeared at Stand Rock for over 30 years.

The Stand Rock Indian Ceremonial has always prided itself on presenting the finest and truest in Indian performers. Since its inception, all of the performers at Stand Rock have been of Native American descent. In 1940 the ceremonial had the distinction of being the only all-Indian show in the country. The Ho-Chunk have presented the main part of the program and groups from other tribes have participated by special invitation. Among those invited have been performers from the Apache, Pueblo and Ojibwe tribes.

While Indians have always performed, it was not until 1987, that the Ho-Chunk assumed entire management of the ceremonial. It has remained an all-Indian operation ever since.

Chief Daybreak, master of ceremonies at Stand Rock for many years.
(Courtesy H.H. Bennett State Historic Site, SHSW)

Dancers at Stand Rock in the 1950s.
(Courtesy H.H. Bennett State Historic Site, SHSW)

DELLS STORIES

No history of Wisconsin Dells would be complete if it did not include H.H. Bennett's stop-action photo of his son Ashley leaping to Stand Rock in 1888.

The studio that H.H. Bennett founded in 1865 has been continuously owned and operated by successive generations of his family. It is the oldest family business in the area and the oldest family-owned photographic studio in the United States.

In 1998, the State Historical Society of Wisconsin announced plans to acquire the Bennett studio, along with its priceless collection of photo prints, negatives and antique equipment. The studio will be restored and become an official state historic site. Although the state will supply some money, most of the funding for the project will come from Wisconsin Dells businesses and individuals committed to preserving a genuine historical treasure in their community.

(Courtesy H.H. Bennett State Historic Site, SHSW)